THE NEW IMMIGRANTS

Filipino Americans
Indian Americans
Jamaican Americans
Korean Americans
Mexican Americans
Ukrainian Americans
Vietnamese Americans

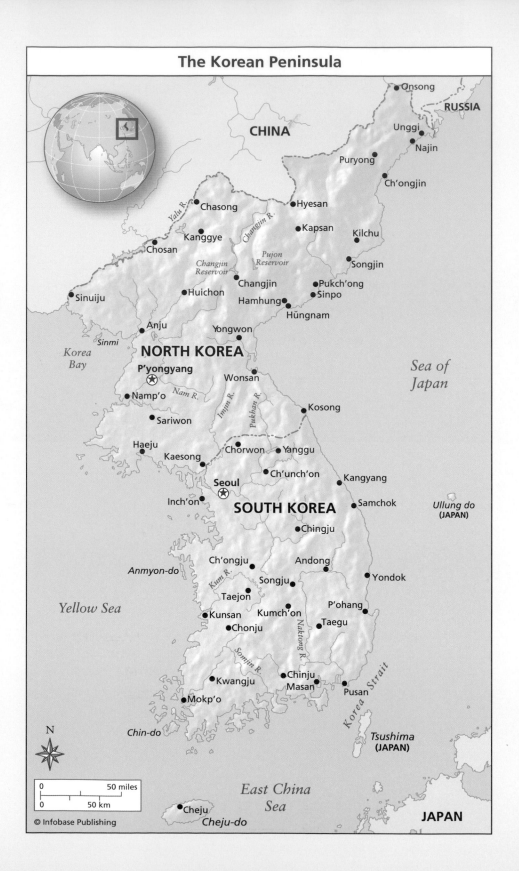

The Korean Peninsula

RUSSIA

CHINA

Onsong

Unggi

Najin

Puryong

Ch'ongjin

Chasong

Hyesan

Kapsan

Kilchu

Yalu R.

Kanggye

Chosan

Changjin R.

Songjin

Changjin
Reservoir

Pujon
Reservoir

Sinuiju

Huichon

Changjin

Pukch'ong

Sinpo

Hamhung

Hŭngnam

Anju

Yongwon

Korea
Bay

Sinmi

NORTH KOREA

P'yongyang

Wonsan

Namp'o

Nam R.

Sea of
Japan

Sariwon

Imjin R.

Pukhan R.

Kosong

Haeju

Chorwon

Yanggu

Kaesong

Ch'unch'on

Kangyang

Seoul

Inch'on

SOUTH KOREA

Samchok

Ullung do
(JAPAN)

Chingju

Ch'ongju

Andong

Yondok

Anmyon-do

Kum R.

Songju

Yellow Sea

Taejon

Kumch'on

P'ohang

Kunsan

Chonju

Naktong R.

Taegu

Somjin R.

Chinju

Kwangju

Masan

Pusan

Korea Strait

Mokp'o

Chin-do

Tsushima
(JAPAN)

N

East China
Sea

JAPAN

0   50 miles

0   50 km

Cheju

Cheju-do

THE NEW IMMIGRANTS

KOREAN
AMERICANS

Anne Soon Choi

Series Editor: Robert D. Johnston
Associate Professor of History,
University of Illinois at Chicago

CHELSEA HOUSE
PUBLISHERS
An imprint of Infobase Publishing

Frontis: Korea is located in East Asia and is home to nearly 72 million people. According to the 2000 U.S. census, approximately 1.3 million people of Korean descent live in the United States.

Korean Americans

Copyright © 2007 by Infobase Publishing

Chelsea House
An imprint of Infobase Publishing
132 West 31st Street
New York NY 10001

Library of Congress Cataloging-in-Publication Data
Choi, Anne Soon.
  Korean Americans / Anne Soon Choi.
    p. cm. — (The new immigrants)
  Includes bibliographical references and index.
  ISBN 0-7910-8788-3 (hardcover)
1. Korean Americans—History—Juvenile literature. 2. Korean Americans—
Social conditions—Juvenile literature. 3. Immigrants—United States—
History—Juvenile literature. 4. Immigrants—United States—Social condi-
tions—Juvenile literature. 5. Korea—Emigration and immigrations—Juvenile
literature. 6. United States—Emigrations and immigrations—Juvenile literature. I. Title.
E184.K6C475 2006
973.'04957—dc   2006019745

Series design by Erika K. Arroyo
Cover design by Takeshi Takahashi

Printed in the United States of America
Bang EJB 10 9 8 7 6 5 4 3 2 1

This book is printed on acid-free paper.

All links and Web addresses were checked and verified to be correct at the time of publication. Because of the dynamic nature of the Web, some addresses and links may have changed since publication and may no longer be valid.

Contents

	Introduction	6
1	Koreans in North America	11
2	The Home Country	21
3	The First Wave: Korean Immigration to Hawaii	33
4	Koreans on the Mainland	44
5	Contemporary Korean Communities in North America	54
6	Korean Adoptees	63
7	Los Angeles, 1992	72
8	Achievements and Challenges for Korean Immigrants	82
9	Notable Korean Americans	98
10	Conclusion	109
	Chronology and Timeline	112
	Notes	115
	Glossary	118
	Bibliography	121
	Further Reading	124
	Index	126

Introduction

Robert D. Johnston

At the time of the publication of this series, there are few more pressing political issues in the country than immigration. Hundreds of thousands of immigrants are filling the streets of major U.S. cities to protect immigrant rights. And conflict in Congress has reached a boiling point, with members of the Senate and House fighting over the proper policy toward immigrants who have lived in the United States for years but who entered the country illegally.

Generally, Republicans and Democrats are split down partisan lines in a conflict of this sort. However, in this dispute, some otherwise conservative Republicans are taking a more liberal position on the immigration issue—precisely because of their own immigrant connections. For example, Pete Domenici, the longest-serving senator in the history of the state of New Mexico, recently told his colleagues about one of the most chilling days of his life.

In 1943, during World War II, the Federal Bureau of Investigation (FBI) set out to monitor U.S. citizens who had ties with Italy, Germany, and Japan. At the time, Domenici was 10 or 11 years old and living in Albuquerque, with his parents—Alda, the president of the local PTA, and Cherubino, an Italian-born grocer who already had become a U.S. citizen. Alda, who had arrived in the United States with her parents when she was three, thought she had her papers in order, but she found out otherwise when federal agents swept in and whisked her away—leaving young Pete in tears.

It turned out that Alda was an illegal immigrant. She was, however, clearly not a security threat, and the government released her on bond. Alda then quickly prepared the necessary paperwork and became a citizen. More than six decades later, her son decided to tell his influential colleagues Alda's story, because, he says, he wanted them to remember that "the sons and daughters of this century's illegal immigrants could end up in the Senate one day, too."[1]

Given the increasing ease of global travel, immigration is becoming a significant political issue throughout the world. Yet the United States remains in many ways the most receptive country toward immigrants that history has ever seen. The Statue of Liberty is still one of our nation's most important symbols.

A complex look at history, however, reveals that, despite the many success stories, there are many more sobering accounts like that of Pete Domenici. The United States has offered unparalleled opportunities to immigrants from Greece to Cuba, Thailand to Poland. Yet immigrants have consistently also suffered from persistent—and sometimes murderous—discrimination.

This series is designed to inform students of both the achievements and the hardships faced by some of the immigrant groups that have arrived in the United States since Congress passed the Immigration and Naturalization Services Act in 1965. The United States was built on the ingenuity and hard work of its nation's immigrants, and these new immigrants—primarily from Asia and

Latin America—have, over the last several decades, added their unique attributes to American culture.

Immigrants from the following countries are featured in THE NEW IMMIGRANTS series: India, Jamaica, Korea, Mexico, the Philippines, Ukraine, and Vietnam. Each book focuses on the present-day life of these ethnic groups—and not just in the United States, but in Canada as well. The books explore their culture, their success in various occupations, the economic hardships they face, and their political struggles. Yet all the authors in the series recognize that we cannot understand any of these groups without also coming to terms with their history—a history that involves not just their time in the United States, but also the lasting legacy of their homelands.

Mexican immigrants, along with their relatives and allies, have been the driving force behind the recent public defense of immigrant rights. Michael Schroeder explains how distinctive the situation of Mexican immigrants is, particularly given the fluid border between the United States and its southern neighbor. Indeed, not only is the border difficult to defend, but some Mexicans (and scholars) see it as an artificial barrier—the result of nineteenth-century imperialist conquest.

Vietnam is perhaps the one country outside of Mexico with the most visible recent connection to the history of the United States. One of the most significant consequences of our tragic war there was a flood of immigrants, most of whom had backed the losing side. Liz Sonneborn demonstrates how the historic conflicts over Communism in the Vietnamese homeland continue to play a role in the United States, more than three decades after the end of the "American" war.

In turn, Filipinos have also been forced out of their native land, but for them economic distress has been the primary cause. Jon Sterngass points out how immigration from the Philippines—as is the case with many Asian countries—reaches back much further in American history than is generally known, with the search for jobs a constant factor.

Koreans who have come to this country also demonstrate just how connected recent immigrants are to their "homelands" while forging a permanent new life in the United States. As Anne Soon Choi reveals, the history of twentieth-century Korea—due to Japanese occupation, division of the country after World War II, and the troubling power of dictators for much of postwar history—played a crucial role in shaping the culture of Korean Americans.

South Asians are, arguably, the greatest source of change in immigration to the United States since 1965. Padma Rangaswamy, an Indian-American scholar and activist, explores how the recent flow of Indians to this country has brought not only delicious food and colorful clothes, but also great technical expertise, as well as success in areas ranging from business to spelling bees.

Jamaican Americans are often best known for their music, as well as for other distinctive cultural traditions. Heather Horst and Andrew Garner show how these traditions can, in part, be traced to the complex and often bitter political rivalries within Jamaica—conflicts that continue to shape the lives of Jamaican immigrants.

Finally, the story of Ukrainian Americans helps us understand that even "white" immigrants suffered considerable hardship, and even discrimination in this land of opportunity. Still, the story that John Radzilowski portrays is largely one of achievement, particularly with the building of successful ethnic communities.

I would like to conclude by mentioning how proud I am to be the editor of this very important series. When I grew up in small-town Oregon during the 1970s, it was difficult to see that immigrants played much of a role in my "white bread" life. Even worse than that ignorance, however, were the lessons I learned from my relatives. They were, unfortunately, quite suspicious of all those they defined as "outsiders." Throughout his life, my grandfather believed that the Japanese who immigrated to his rural valley in central Oregon were helping Japan during World War II by collecting scrap from gum wrappers to make weapons. My uncles, who were also fruit growers, were openly hostile toward the Mexican immigrants without whom they could not have harvested their apples and pears.

Fortunately, like so many other Americans, the great waves of immigration since 1965 have taught me to completely rethink my conception of America. I live in Chicago, a block from Devon Avenue, one of the primary magnets of Indian and Pakistani immigrations in this country (Padma Rangaswamy mentions Devon in her fine book in this series on Indian Americans). Conversely, when my family and I lived in Storm Lake, Iowa, in the early 1990s, immigrants from Laos, Mexico, and Somalia were also decisively reshaping the face of that small town. Throughout America, we live in a new country—one not without problems, but one that is incredibly exciting and vibrant. I hope that this series helps you appreciate even more one of the most special qualities of the American heritage.

Note

1. Rachel L. Swarns, "An Immigration Debate Framed by Family Ties," *New York Times,* April 4, 2006.

Robert D. Johnston
Chicago, Illinois
April 2006

1

Koreans in North America

Born in 1900, Mary Paik Lee immigrated to America with her family in 1905. The family was part of the earliest wave of Korean immigrants to North America. The Paik's experience, like those of other immigrants to the United States and Canada, is a story of struggle and hardship, as well as one of opportunity and success. Most important, though, it is about ordinary people who had to make difficult decisions as they left everything they knew to begin a new life in a new land. In describing her family's decision to migrate to the United States, Mary Paik Lee put it this way:

> Mother told me there had been a lot of discussion for several days before the final decision was made for my parents to leave Korea to find a better life elsewhere. Father was reluctant to leave, but his parents insisted, saying that his presence would not help them. They

knew what would happen to them in the near future. They were prepared to face great hardship or worse, but they wanted at least one member of their family to survive and live a better life somewhere else. Such strong, quiet courage in ordinary people in the face of danger is really something to admire and remember always.[1]

This desire to "live a better life" has been one of the central forces behind Korean immigration throughout the twentieth century. The earliest Korean immigrants were recruited to work in the sugarcane fields in Hawaii around 1900. Like other Asian immigrant groups of this time period, including Japanese and Chinese immigrants, Koreans experienced discrimination from mainstream society because of their racial and cultural differences. At the same time, in the first half of the century,

Number of Immigrants Admitted to the United States from Korea, 1949–2004

Year of Entry	Number Admitted
1820–1948*	—
1949–1950	107
1951–1960	6,231
1961–1970	34,526
1971–1980	267,638
1981–1990	333,746
1991–2000	164,166
2001–2004	71,665

*Prior to 1949, immigration data for Korean Americans was not reported separately.

Source: Department of Homeland Security Web site. Available online at *http://www.uscis.gov/graphics/shared/statistics/year-book/2004/table2.xls*

the experiences of Korean immigrants were unique: In addition to the struggle of adjusting to a new country, Koreans had to face the occupation of their homeland by Japan. As a result, for Koreans in North America, the struggle to free their homeland from Japanese colonial rule through the Korean independence movement was a powerful force, until 1945, when Japan was defeated in World War II.

It is also important to understand how "place" mattered for the first wave of Korean immigrants. The experiences of Korean immigrants in Hawaii differed greatly from their counterparts on the mainland. This difference was the result of a number of factors. In Hawaii, given the dynamics of labor migration, Asian immigrants significantly outnumbered whites, which

Ronald Moon, chief justice of the Hawaii State Supreme Court, is a third-generation Korean American—both of his grandparents came to Hawaii during the first wave of immigration from 1903 to 1905. In 2003, Moon was one of many Korean Americans who celebrated the centennial of his people's initial immigration to the United States.

I AM KOREAN

In the eventful days following Japan's bombing of Pearl Harbor on December 7, 1941, which marked the entry of the United States into World War II, the response of Korean immigrant communities in Hawaii and California ranged from fear to hopefulness. Koreans in America were hopeful because U.S. entry into the war against Japan could potentially mean the liberation of their homeland from Japanese colonial rule. At the same time, Korean immigrants found themselves in a difficult situation for two reasons: (1) They were classified as "enemy aliens," because they were considered Japanese subjects. (2) They were denied U.S. citizenship, because of revisions to U.S. immigration law in the decades before World War II.

As a result, Korean immigrants during World War II struggled to distinguish themselves from the Japanese. This was a difficult task, as the majority of Americans thought of Asian immigrants as "one and the same," and could not tell the difference between various Asian nationalities. One way Korean immigrants distinguished themselves from the Japanese was to engage in anti-Japanese activities. As one observer noted in the 1930s about the Koreans, "Singly and collectively they hate the Japanese; all Japanese."* During World War II, to demonstrate their anti-Japanese feelings and to make sure that they would not be confused with the Japanese, Koreans in the United States wore buttons that declared, "I am Korean."

Like many other countries during the first half of the twentieth century, Korea found itself under the colonial rule of a more powerful nation. Unwillingly colonized by Japan in 1910, the struggle

created a very different social dynamic. Also in this time period, the Korean population in Hawaii was much larger than on the mainland. On the eve of World War II, there were about 9,000

for independence emerged as a significant organizing force in Korea and in Korean immigrant communities throughout the world. Kyung-Soo Cha recalled being a little girl in Korea:

> *I didn't know what the word "independence" meant, so one day I asked my mother. "The adults these days talk about independence a lot. What does it mean?" My mother replied, "The Japanese came to our country to exploit and rule us. Independence means that we can live by ourselves. Don't let anyone hear you saying the word. The Japanese will catch you and beat you."***

Korean immigrants in the United States, especially in Hawaii and the American West, played a central role in the struggle for Korean liberation. This was due to the fact that Korean immigrants to the United States had political freedom and economic opportunity, which their counterparts in Korea, who lived under a system of repressive colonial rule, did not have. This political situation in Asia guaranteed that Koreans in the United States would eagerly support the U.S. military action against Japan as a way to secure Korean independence. Although Korean immigrant communities were actively involved in the politics of their homeland, though, it is also important to keep in mind that Korean immigrants were deeply invested in their lives in the United States. Even in a period of profound anti-Asian discrimination, Koreans struggled to demonstrate that they could be both Korean and American.

---

  * Quoted in Ronald Takaki, *Strangers from A Different Shore: A History of Asian Americans* (Boston: Little, Brown and Company, 1989), 281.
** Kyung-Cha Cha, *Pumpkin Flower and Patriotism* (Los Angeles: Korean American Research Center, 1991), 27.

Korean immigrants in Hawaii, whereas on the mainland, the Korean population (largely concentrated in Southern California) numbered about 1,200.

Today, Koreans are one of the largest and most visible Asian immigrant groups in North America. Korean communities exist not only in major cities like Chicago, New York, Los Angeles, and Toronto but also in unexpected places like Memphis and Atlanta. Korean settlement over a wide area resulted from a number of factors, including patterns of post-1965 immigration to North America, economic opportunity, and historic ties between the United States, Canada, and Korea. At the same time, it is important to remember that the history of Korean immigrants dates to the early part of the twentieth century. Thus, Korean immigration can be best understood in two distinct waves, pre-1965 and post-1965.

THE POLITICS OF EXCLUSION

Asian immigrants, in addition to the struggles of adapting to a new country, language, and culture, also faced racial discrimination. Discrimination targeting Asian immigrants dated to the nineteenth century and the movement to exclude the Chinese from the United States. As large numbers of Chinese immigrants entered California with the discovery of gold at Sutter's Mill in 1848, native-born whites saw Chinese immigrants as an economic threat. Employers were eager to embrace a Chinese immigrant labor force that was willing to work long hours for low wages, but the use of Chinese labor threatened the livelihood of working-class whites. Chinese immigrants were also viewed negatively because of their visible racial difference. Those supporting Chinese exclusion argued that Asians could not assimilate into American life. In 1869, Henry George, a prominent journalist, argued:

> The Chinese have a civilization and history of their own; a vanity which causes them to look down on all other races, habits of thought rendered permanent by being stamped upon countless generations. From present appearances we shall have a permanent Chinese population. . . . A population born in China, expecting to return to China,

living here in a little China of its own, and with the slightest attachment to the country—utter heathens, treacherous, sensual, cowardly, and cruel.[2]

The anti-Chinese movement originated on the West Coast, but it quickly became a national phenomenon, as well as a campaign to exclude Chinese immigrant laborers. This campaign resulted in the 1882 Chinese Exclusion Act, the first American immigration policy that excluded any group of individuals based on race and national origin. Significantly, the *Chinese Exclusion Act* ultimately became the foundation

Large-scale immigration to the United States by Korean Americans did not occur until Congress passed the Immigration and Naturalization Services Act of 1965. The act abolished the national quota system established by the Immigration Act of 1924. As a result, many Koreans settled in cities such as San Francisco. Pictured here is a group of Korean Americans who are welcoming then-Korean President Chung Hee Park at San Francisco's Moffett Naval Air Station in August 1969.

and model for the exclusion of nearly all Asian immigrants by the 1920s.

With the ban on Chinese labor, employers turned to the Japanese as a reliable source of labor. Anti-Asian sentiment was expanded, then, to include the Japanese, and Japanese laborers were excluded through the *Gentlemen's Agreement of 1907*. Unlike the Chinese, however, who were singled out by name in the 1882 Chinese Exclusion Act, by the early part of the twentieth century, Japan had emerged as a world power. Consequently, it was difficult for the United States to single out Japanese immigrants in the same way as the Chinese had been singled out, and this resulted in the carefully worded "Gentlemen's Agreement." The anti-Asian sentiment of this agreement was clear, however.

In the push for the exclusion of Japanese and Korean immigrants, the Asiatic Exclusion League declared: "The nations of Asia are nations apart from those of the West, nor do they wish to be otherwise. The Asiatic can never be other than an Asiatic, however much he may imitate the dress of the white man, nor will he ever have the slightest concern for our laws, except to evade them; nor with the Government, except to cajole and deceive it."[3]

Although no specific law excluded Korean immigrants by name, because of the colonization of Korea by Japan in 1910, Koreans in the United States were classified as Japanese nationals and were barred by the 1907 Gentlemen's Agreement. As a result, the first period of Korean migration was quite brief. Both the Chinese Exclusion Act of 1882 and the 1907 Gentlemen's Agreement, however, singled out laborers and left a loophole for students, diplomats, merchants, and the wives of men already in the United States. For Korean immigration, this loophole was very important, especially for the continued migration of women and students. Anti-immigration sentiment, in general, escalated in the United States in the early part of the twentieth century, and the loophole was closed by the *Immigration Act of 1924*. This act established a quota system based on national origin and prohibited all Asian immigration. As a result, mass Asian immigration was halted until the *Immigration and Naturalization Services Act of 1965*, which dismantled the quota system.

When Korean independence came in 1945 (Japan had controlled Korea since 1910) as a result of the Allied Powers' defeat of Japan during World War II, the majority of Korean immigrants remained in the United States and formed the foundation for future immigration. The 1950s witnessed new Korean immigration to the United States, including military brides, orphans, and college students. Mass Korean immigration did not begin until after 1965, however, with the dramatic change in American immigration policy. The mass migration of Koreans to the United States profoundly changed American society in a number of ways. The influx of Asian immigrants changed the way that race was discussed and analyzed in the United States. In addition, settlement of Korean immigrants in urban areas had a significant impact on regional economies as Koreans began to dominate particular economic niches. It also caused conflict, most notably between Koreans and African Americans, which was infamously documented in the media coverage of the *1992 Los Angeles Riots*.

Although the context of contemporary Korean immigration is very different from earlier waves of Korean migration, post-1965 immigrants share many of the same experiences as earlier Korean immigrants. These experiences included the difficulties of adapting to a new country and the promises of opportunity.

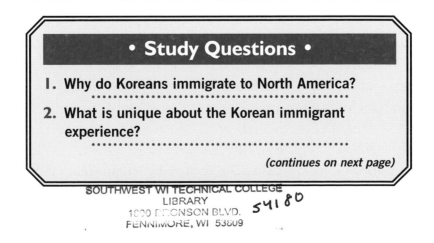

• Study Questions •

1. Why do Koreans immigrate to North America?
....
2. What is unique about the Korean immigrant experience?
....

(continues on next page)

(continued from previous page)

3. What is significant about the 1882 Chinese Exclusion Act?

    ....

4. What prompted anti-Asian feelings in the United States?

    ....

5. How were Koreans excluded from immigrating to the United States?

    ....

2

The Home Country

According to legend, a very long time ago, a she-bear and a tigress who lived in a cave together prayed to Hwanung, the son of heaven, to become human. Moved by their prayers, he provided them with special food—20 cloves of garlic and herbs—and instructed them to stay out of sunlight for 100 days. Finding this too difficult, the tigress quickly gave up. The she-bear persevered, however, and in 21 days, she was transformed into a woman. The woman was overjoyed at first, but without a companion, she became increasingly sad. So, she prayed under a sandalwood tree for a child. Again, Hwanung was moved by her prayers and made her his wife, and she soon bore a son. They named him *Tangun*, which means "sandalwood."

Tangun grew into a wise and powerful leader and founded Gojoseon, the land of the morning calm in 2333 B.C. He ruled benevolently, and Gojoseon prospered. Tangun is recognized as the founder of Korea.

Gojoseon, like other less-powerful kingdoms in the region, eventually fell under Chinese control. (Korea borders China to the north and west.) Thus began a long period of Chinese influence on the Korean Peninsula. By the third century A.D., however, the Chinese were defeated, and a number of competing states emerged. The geographic region today known as Korea emerged in the tenth century with the unification of three kingdoms—Paekche, Silla, and Koguryo.

THE HERMIT KINGDOM

The unification of the Korean Peninsula did not change the fact that Korea existed in the shadow of her more powerful neighbors. One important strategy that Korea adopted to maintain its sovereignty was to establish a close relationship with China, beginning in the fourteenth century, where Korea paid tribute to China. Consequently, as a "little brother" of China, Korea remained independent and benefited from China's protection. Korea attempted to maintain its position by closing its borders to all trade and travel except that with China, which earned Korea the nickname of the "Hermit Kingdom."

This close relationship between the two countries placed Korea within the Chinese world order.[4] China's impact on Korea cannot be underestimated—the relationship affected political institutions and cultural influences, and introduced *Confucianism* and Buddhism to Korea. Despite China's influence, however, Korea maintained its own cultural and political identity.

The "big brother–little brother" relationship between China and Korea lasted well into the nineteenth century. Eventually, however, enormous change came to Asia. The combination of internal political unrest and the "opening" of China by Western countries weakened China's position in Asia. This, combined with the modernization of Japan and Japan's interest in territorial expansion, left Korea in a vulnerable position.

CONFUCIANISM IN KOREA

Confucianism has been one of the most important and long-lasting influences in Korea. It was introduced to Korea from China during the Three Kingdoms period, beginning in 1 B.C. Specifically, Confucianism as a belief system provides a clear guide for all relationships: between rulers and subjects, husbands and wives, parents and children, and elders and youth. Thus, Confucianism emphasizes proper and harmonious social relationships in all aspects of life, including government, the legal system, the family, and society. It allowed Korea to maintain a stable sociopolitical system on the peninsula and, in general, peaceful relations with her more powerful neighbors.

Confucianism in Korea thrived during the Joseon Dynasty (A.D. 1392–1910). Not only did its belief system serve as the guiding principles that governed the yangban (elite) class, but it had a profound influence on Korean culture: During this period, an exam system for civil service was established and encouraged artistic and literary endeavors.

At the end of the nineteenth century, Confucianism in Korea went into decline with the collapse of China's Qing Dynasty and the entry of Western countries into Asia. In addition, the colonization of Korea by Japan (1910–1945) also worked to diminish the influence of Confucian thought on the Korean Peninsula.

Today, it is clear that Confucianism still maintains an important influence in Korea, particularly in the arts. The impact of Confucianism can also still be seen in the organization of Korean society, with its emphasis on hierarchy and proper social relationships, both in public and private life.

Korea's worst fears came true in the early part of the twentieth century, as Japan emerged as a world power after defeating China in the Sino-Japanese War in 1895 and Russia in the Russo-Japanese War in 1905. By 1910, Japan had made Korea into a Japanese colony.

During the late 1800s, Japan emerged as a world power and began expanding its territorial holdings in Asia. By 1910, Japan forced Korea to sign the Japan-Korea Annexation Treaty, which formally ceded Korea to Japan. Japanese gendarmes (police officers), such as the ones pictured in this 1910 photograph, often meted out punishment against those Koreans who spoke out against Japanese rule.

KOREA UNDER JAPANESE RULE

For Japan, the colonization of Korea was the first step in the expansion of the Japanese empire. Although on the international stage, Japan declared that the colonization was in the best interest of Korea, in reality, Japanese colonial rule was brutal and violent. Koreans were forced to adopt Japanese names, speaking Korean was prohibited, and Korean natural resources were exported to feed the growing Japanese empire. Koreans were made second-class citizens in their own country. One woman recalled:

By Summer, 1917, many Koreans had a beaten, frightened, searching look. Now there were thousands of Japanese civilians in our country. Wealth was being drained out of Korea. Many of our rich friends were becoming poorer and poorer every year. And the poor were pushed toward starvation. Greedy Japanese seized the richest rice fields. When they needed shelter, they took Korean homes. Our railroads and banks fell before the economic onslaught.[5]

Koreans did not accept colonization passively. Despite the brutality of Japanese rule, Koreans resisted colonization as much as possible. The Korean independence movement was the most visible resistance. Not only did Koreans struggle for freedom in their own country, but those who had immigrated to China, Manchuria, and the United States emerged as crucial players in the independence movement.

The most dramatic moment in the independence movement came in 1919—the *March First Incident*. The death of King Gojong, the last emperor of Korea, provided an opportunity for Koreans to demonstrate their anti-Japanese feelings in a peaceful mass demonstration. The Japanese colonial government allowed Koreans to pay their respects to King Gojong as he lay in state in Seoul, the country's capital. During this mass demonstration, the Korean Declaration of Independence was read. An estimated 2 million Koreans took part in these peaceful demonstrations. The Japanese response was swift and brutal, however, as an estimated 7,500 Koreans were killed and 45,000 arrested throughout the country. This violent political repression against those who worked for Korean independence was echoed by Min-ja Sur, a schoolteacher, who described the response of the Japanese to the March First Movement of 1919: "The Japanese went crazy. They beat up people and killed thousands of Koreans while many were arrested and later killed."[6]

The March First Incident was a critical turning point for Korean freedom. International outrage forced Japan to reconsider its colonial policies. It also began a new period of activity in the Korean independence movement in Korea and overseas. Outside Korea, Korean independence activities included guerrilla attacks along the Manchurian-Korean border, the establishment of an exile Korean government in China, and diplomatic efforts and financial support from the United States. In the end, the defeat of Japan at the end of World War II liberated Korea.

THE TWO KOREAS

Although the end of the war in 1945 brought freedom from Japan, it was only the beginning of Korea's trouble. Years of colonial rule left Korea in ruins. As a temporary measure, Korea was divided into two occupational zones, with the Soviet Union in the north and the United States in the south, until a plan for rebuilding Korea could be worked out. This division was met by outrage by Koreans everywhere, all of whom demanded a unified Korea.

The hopes for a unified Korea quickly disappeared as pro-Communist and anti-Communist politics came into play. In 1948, two separate nations—with opposing political and social beliefs—were established with the division of the Korean Peninsula at the 38th parallel into North Korea (*Democratic Peoples Republic of Korea*) and South Korea (*Republic of Korea*).

In 1950, the outbreak of the *Korean War* ended any hopes for reunification. This civil war was at one level about reunifying the peninsula, but it was also about the larger dynamics of the cold war, as the Soviet Union and China became allies of North Korea and the United States and United Nations sided with South Korea. Nearly three years of battle and destruction did little to resolve the conflict on the peninsula.

The Korean War (1950 to 1953) greatly affected both North and South Korea—more than 2 million Koreans lost their lives in the conflict and the infrastructure of both countries was virtually destroyed. Pictured here are residents of Pyongyang, North Korea, fleeing across a damaged bridge that crosses the Taedong River in advance of Chinese Communist troops in December 1950.

The cost of the war was enormous. More than 2 million Koreans from the north and the south lost their lives. This was in addition to the massive loss of life of Chinese and American military forces. The war, which was fought on the peninsula, virtually destroyed the infrastructure of North and South Korea, including roads, bridges, government houses, schools, and private homes.

The war failed to reunite the peninsula and, in fact, hardened the division between North and South Korea. Despite being referred to as the demilitarized zone (DMZ), the border between the two Koreas is one of the most militarized regions in the world. In proportion to its population, North Korea has one of the world's largest military forces, and U.S. troops are still a significant presence in South Korea. To date, the war is technically not over, because a peace treaty was never signed.

NORTH KOREA

Today, North Korea, with a population of 22 million, is one of the most isolated and mysterious countries in the world. It is considered the last truly Communist country. Led by Kim Il Sung, a former guerrilla leader, North Korea was an important part of the cold war world order from 1948 until his death in 1994. Supported politically and financially by China and the Soviet Union, North Korea maintains its Communist regime. Its reliance on China and the Soviet Union increasingly isolated North Korea from international trade and credit, however. At the same time, the escalating conflict between the Soviet Union and China left North Korea in a vulnerable position. North Korea's isolation was further compounded by a political system built around Kim Il Sung and his son Kim Jong-il, who officially became the leader of North Korea in 1997.

Kim Jong-il's rise to power in the 1990s corresponded with the steady deterioration of the North Korean economy and the general decline in the standard of living. This deterioration was further compounded by mass famine between

1996 and 1999, which resulted in nearly one million deaths and untold suffering. Gerald Bourke, a representative of the United Nation's (UN's) World Food Program, described the desperation of North Koreans as they turned to seaweed and grass as a food source: "You see people of all ages going up into the hillsides with bags and sacks and coming back down with grasses. You see women on the seashores scavenging for edible seaweeds."[7]

The crisis of the famine forced North Korea to open its borders to organizations such as the Red Cross and the United Nations. Although mass starvation was avoided, reports indicate that North Korea, despite its refusal to acknowledge its internal problems, is in crisis. In addition, despite the massive aid provided by the West, South Korea, and Japan, the North Korean government has continued its hostile criticism of these countries.

Because of the isolation of North Korea and its strict monitoring and control of foreign visitors, until recently very little was known about daily life in the Communist nation. The combination of famine and a repressive government, however, prompted a number of North Koreans to defect to China, with South Korea as their final destination. North Korean defectors often recount tales of oppression and brutality in North Korea. A Communist party official who had smuggled a radio from China to listen to music learned that someone had revealed his secret. He said, "It could have been my children who said something outside. It could have been my friend; no one knew. If a farmer or laborer had a radio, he could have been released. But I was an official. In my case, it would have been torture and a life sentence in a political prisoners' camp."[8] Faced with such a response, he chose to save his life. He left his wife and two small children and crossed into China, where he spent three years as a fugitive until Christian missionaries helped him make his way to South Korea.

Although the immediate crisis of famine has passed, the future of North Korea is uncertain. After the terrorist events of September 11, 2001, there is concern over North Korea's nuclear arms program and its impact on the political and economic stability of the region, which includes China, Japan, and South Korea.

SOUTH KOREA

South Korea has an equally complicated history. The country was occupied by the United States after World War II. Then, in 1948, the U.S. government brought Syngman Rhee to power. Rhee was a key leader in the Korean independence movement in the United States. He was forced to resign, however, in the face of massive student uprisings that protested his undemocratic policies in the 1960s. A brief period of civil rule was brought to an end when Park Chung Hee established a dictatorship in South Korea through a military coup. The dictatorship lasted until Hee was assassinated in 1979. Significantly, under Hee's rule, South Korea began its dramatic economic growth; however, civil unrest against the repressive military government continued. After Hee's assassination in 1979, though, a process of political reform—one that would establish a genuine democracy in South Korea—finally began.

By the 1990s, South Korea had emerged as one of the world's largest economies. The country has become known for brands such as Hyundai, Samsung, and LG, as well as the production of automobiles, cell phones, and a wide range of electronic goods. Currently, with a population of 48 million, South Korea is the world's eleventh-largest economy. In addition, South Korea is one of the most wired nations in the world, with inexpensive and mass access to the Internet.

South Korea has made its mark on the world in a number of ways. In Asia, South Korea is home to a large number of Christians, nearly a third of its population. South Korean immigrants have settled throughout the world. Culturally,

South Koreans have excelled in world sports, including soccer and golf. Korean soap operas have gained worldwide popularity, and Korean films have been met with critical acclaim.

CURRENT SITUATION

Although attempts have been made on the part of South Korea to ease the tensions between the two countries, there has been little progress. The most publicized and moving effort has been the family reunion campaigns, where families separated by the Korean War were briefly allowed to reunite.

The following is an account of one such reunion:

"Sister Shin-ho! Sister Shin-ho! You are alive," her younger South Korean sister, Bu-ja, cried, as they embraced. Bu-ja attended the reunion in the place of their 93-year-old mother, who died two days earlier. "Until the moment of her death, our mother could never close her eyes peacefully without seeing you," Bu-ja told her sister. Lee Shin-ho sobbed as she knelt in front of a portrait of their mother.[9]

At the same time, it is clear, especially in the aftermath of a devastating famine in the late 1990s and from the accounts of North Koreans who have defected to the south, that the North Korean regime cannot maintain its current position and policies. This is of great concern to China and South Korea, the countries that would be forced to take in North Korean refugees if North Korea should collapse. North Korea has also gained attention for its nuclear program and has been declared a part of the "axis of evil" by President George W. Bush.

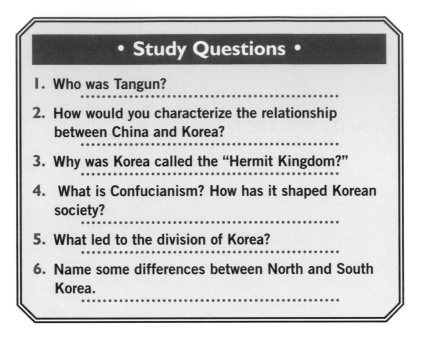

• Study Questions •

1. Who was Tangun?

2. How would you characterize the relationship between China and Korea?

3. Why was Korea called the "Hermit Kingdom?"

4. What is Confucianism? How has it shaped Korean society?

5. What led to the division of Korea?

6. Name some differences between North and South Korea.

3

The First Wave:
Korean Immigration to Hawaii

In the early part of the twentieth century, the *picture bride* system was established to allow single Korean and Japanese men to marry at a time when Japanese and Korean laborers were prohibited from entering the United States due to the 1907 Gentlemen's Agreement. The law left a loophole open for wives and families of Japanese and Korean immigrant men already in the United States to enter the country. Thus, potential brides exchanged photos with their prospective husbands, and if all was agreeable, the couple was "married" in Korea by having the bride's name entered in the husband's family register. Once they were married, these picture brides could apply for passports to join their husbands in the United States. The picture bride system allowed for the emigration of more than 20,000 Japanese women and 1,200 Korean women in the first two decades of the twentieth century. Once American immigration officials caught on to the practice, though, the picture bride system came to an end. All loopholes for Asian immigration were closed off with the Immigration Act of 1924. One Korean immigrant picture bride (see sidebar below) explained her reasons for emigrating from Korea:

> My parents were very poor. One year, a heavy rain came, a flood, the crops all washed down. Oh it was a very hard time. . . . Under the Japanese, no freedom. Not even free talking. Hawaii's a free place, everybody living well. Hawaii had freedom, so if you like talk, you can talk; you like work, you can work. I want to come,

PICTURE BRIDES

One Korean immigrant woman recalled her initial response, as a 15-year-old picture bride, to meeting her husband for the first time: "When I first saw my husband, I could not believe my eyes. His hair was grey and I could not see any resemblance to the picture I had. He was forty-six years old."*

Like this young bride who expressed shock at her much older husband when she saw him for the first time, many picture brides found themselves married to men several years their senior. Many men who desperately wanted a wife oftentimes resorted to deception. Not only did they send pictures of themselves at a younger age, but they sometimes substituted photos of younger men. Lying about their age was not the only way these men deceived prospective wives. Many sent photos of themselves posing with cars and houses they did not own or in rented or borrowed suits. Consequently, many picture brides found themselves not only with much older men but with working-class men with meager resources.

Faced with the choice of settling down with husbands they had never seen or returning to Korea, the vast majority of Korean picture brides, for better or for worse, chose to stay in Hawaii. As wives of laborers, many Korean picture brides found themselves

so, I sent my picture. Ah marriage! Then I could go to America! That land of freedom with streets paved of gold! Since I became ten, I've been forbidden to step outside our gates, just like the rest of the girls of my days. So becoming a picture bride would be my answer and release.[10]

Like this picture bride, the earliest Korean immigrants came to America for economic, political, and individual opportunity. Beginning in 1903, the first Koreans arrived in Hawaii aboard the S.S. *Gaelic*. Recruited as labor for the sugar plantations,

working side by side with their husbands in the sugarcane fields. One woman recalled,

> *The sugar cane fields were endless and the stalks were twice the height of myself. Now that I look back, I thank goodness for the height, for if I had seen how far the fields stretched, I probably would have fainted from knowing how much work was ahead. My waistline got slimmer and my back ached from bending over all the time to cut the sugar cane.***

Picture brides were essential to Korean immigrant communities, given the gender imbalance of Korean migrants. Picture brides not only contributed their labor, but they also ensured that a second generation of Korean Americans was possible and that the growth of Korean immigrant communities would continue.

---

* Quoted in Ronald Takaki, *Strangers From a Different Shore: A History of Asian Americans* (Boston: Little, Brown, 1989), 72.
** Ibid., 137.

these 120 immigrants would be joined by more than 7,000 other immigrants, the vast majority of them men, to meet the demands of the Hawaiian sugar industry. The window for Korean immigration, about three years, was brief in comparison to that of other Asian immigrant groups, however. Anti-Asian immigrant sentiment in the United States, which first targeted Chinese immigrants, quickly expanded to include Japanese and Korean immigrants. Koreans were excluded from immigration to the United States through the 1907 Gentlemen's Agreement. The agreement banned the immigration of Japanese laborers, and by 1905 Japan had made it clear to the world that Korea would eventually be incorporated into the growing Japanese empire.

LEAVING THE LAND OF THE MORNING CALM

Similar to the experiences of other American immigrants, a number of "push-and-pull" factors contributed to the migration of Koreans. The late nineteenth century brought enormous change to Asia, and Korea was not exempt. Historically, Korea, a small mountainous nation, had been at the mercy of her larger and more powerful neighbors, China and Japan. This was true in the late nineteenth century, too. As mentioned previously, China, Korea's protector for hundreds of years, became weaker politically, and Korea was left vulnerable to the territorial expansion of Japan, which in turn created political instability in Korea. By 1910, Japan's territorial interest in Korea turned into formal occupation, and Korea was made a Japanese colony. Colonization brought enormous hardship to Korea as Japan exploited Korean natural resources and labor. A central strategy of Japan in gaining control over Korea was to steadily dismantle Korean culture and identity. Consequently, the desire for political freedom emerged as a significant "push" factor for Korean immigrants, especially for those who believed that they could work for Korean independence in the United States. One

During the early 1900s, Japanese colonization and the resultant poverty it created forced many Koreans to leave their homeland and immigrate to the United States. Many East Asian immigrants, including Koreans, entered the United States at Angel Island, California, which is pictured here.

immigrant declared, "When I saw my country fall into the hands of the Japanese aggressors, I was filled with sorrow, but, unable to do much to help, I applied for the status of an immigrant and came to Hawai'i hoping to learn something in order to help my country."[11]

At the same time, as it was for other Asian immigrants, poverty was a significant "push" factor that encouraged Korean immigration in the early part of the twentieth century. A cycle of famine and drought created enormous hardship for many ordinary Koreans, and as a result, immigrating to Hawaii looked attractive. One Korean immigrant recalled, "We had nothing to eat. There was absolutely no way we could survive. There were no opportunities for work of any kind and conditions were bad. It was then that we heard of a man who was talking a lot about the opportunities in Hawai'i. He said it was a land of opportunity where everybody was rich."[12]

As for "pull" factors, in the latter part of the nineteenth century, the U.S. demand for sugar increased dramatically. Rather than importing sugar at a higher cost from the Caribbean, American businessmen turned to the tropical climate of Hawaii, an American territory, to expand the small sugar industry that was already in place. The cultivation of sugar required a large, reliable labor force for the harvesting of sugarcane and processing of sugarcane into sugar.

At first, Chinese immigrants were imported as contract laborers. The contract labor system paid a worker the cost of travel to the United States. He or she would then spend an agreed amount of time working off the cost of passage. Given the backbreaking nature of harvesting and processing sugarcane, it is not surprising that many Chinese refused to renew their contracts. In response, the Hawaiian Sugar Planters' Association (HSPA) recruited Japanese laborers in significant numbers. Again, the HSPA found that many Japanese, like the Chinese, were reluctant to renew their contracts and instead sought better employment opportunities on the mainland. In addition, the large number of Japanese laborers concentrated in the sugar industry in the Hawaiian Islands led to labor unrest. This unrest took the form of massive strikes, as these workers demanded better pay and better working conditions. In an effort to solve the problem and prevent similar problems in the future, the HSPA sought non-Japanese laborers as strikebreakers. It was at this point that recruiting Korean labor became necessary.

Missionaries were the critical link between the HSPA and Korean migrants. Korean immigrants in the early part of the twentieth century were unusual in that the vast majority who emigrated were Christians. Not only did

American missionaries have ties to sugar planters in Hawaii, but they actively encouraged Korean Christians to migrate to a Christian land, where it would be easier to cultivate and maintain their newfound faith. At the same time, the conditions in Korea had worsened. The push factors—the prospect of Japanese colonization, famine in the northern regions of Korea, and political and economic instability—combined with the pull factors—financial opportunities, political freedom, and steady employment—set the stage for mass Korean emigration.

Another factor that enticed Koreans to leave their homeland was the availability of jobs on Hawaiian sugar plantations. Christian missionaries played a large role in encouraging Korean Christians to immigrate to the United States, where they could openly practice their religion. Pictured here are workers harvesting sugarcane on the Hawaiian island of Oahu in the 1940s.

KOREANS IN HAWAII

Unlike other immigrant groups in the United States, Korean immigrants in Hawaii at first found themselves isolated. On one level, this isolation was attributable to the geography of the Hawaiian Islands and the distribution of workers on sugar plantations. On another level, the HSPA made sure to disperse Koreans throughout the plantations, to prevent labor organization.

No matter how scattered Koreans were around the islands, however, they still managed to form tight-knit communities, generally organized around a church. Indeed, the Protestant Church has served as a powerful organizing institution for Korean immigrants throughout the twentieth century. This is not surprising. One defining feature of Korean immigration was the significant number of immigrants who had already converted to Christianity. This was due to the strong presence of Protestant missionaries in the nineteenth century, who had worked to establish Christianity in Korea by founding churches and religiously affiliated schools and hospitals. It is important to note, that, in the early period of Korean immigration, the vast majority of immigrants migrated to the United States through Protestant missionary networks.

Despite the influence of both Presbyterian and Methodist missionaries in Korea, the majority of Korean immigrants in the 1910s and 1920s in Hawaii and on the mainland were Methodist. George Heber Jones, a Methodist missionary in Korea, encouraged many of his parishioners to journey to America.[13] Korean immigrants also established other Protestant denominational churches. For Korean immigrants, the church met the spiritual needs of its members, but it also served other functions as well. The church was the social center of Korean immigrant life, because Sunday was the one free day that Koreans had from the grinding labor of the plantations. For new immigrants, the church provided the resources needed to settle into life in the United States. In times of need, the church provided financial assistance. The church also served as the center of the U.S.-based element of the Korean independence movement.

The mass migration of Koreans from 1903 to 1905 predated the formal colonization of Korea in 1910. The crisis of colonization transformed Koreans abroad into passionate political activists who worked tirelessly for Korean liberation. Although all Koreans had the shared goal of Korean independence, Korean political leaders in Hawaii had varying ideas of how to achieve this goal. Park Youngman and Syngman Rhee were the most visible of these political leaders. Youngman argued for a buildup of an overseas military force that would join Koreans in China to drive the Japanese out of Korea. Syngman Rhee, who would go on to be the first president of South Korea, advocated diplomatic means for Korean independence. Unfortunately, the personality conflicts between Syngman Rhee and Park Youngman and others, and the significantly different approaches to the question of Korean independence, sharply divided the Korean community in Hawaii.

Like other Asian immigrants, Koreans sought other opportunities once their contracts expired. More than 1,000 Koreans immigrated to the mainland before laws were put in place to keep Asian immigrants in Hawaii, because of their importance to the labor force. The modernization of the sugar industry soon ended the need for so many workers, however. As a result, many Koreans became involved in the cultivation of coffee and pineapples. They also opened their own businesses, which included restaurants, laundries, and general stores.

For the second generation, the American-born children of Korean immigrants, Hawaii offered unique opportunities. Unlike on the mainland, where anti-Asian sentiment was a part of daily life, in Hawaii this attitude was far more muted: Asian immigrants significantly outnumbered whites and formed the largest racial group in the islands. Whites, however, controlled the majority of economic and political institutions. In the 1930s and 1940s, as American citizens, many second-genera-tion Koreans in Hawaii not only attended college, but, because of the racial composition in Hawaii and the size of the Korean community, they had the opportunity to become professionals. This was in stark contrast to the experiences of second-genera-tion Koreans on the mainland, who found few opportunities for professional careers.

This is not to suggest that Hawaii was free of anti-Asian discrimination. The second-class status of Asian immigrants would become painfully clear with the bombing of Pearl Har-bor and the beginning of World War II in 1941.

Significantly, the relatively large size of the Korean immigrant community in Hawaii, especially in Honolulu, also provided Korean parents more opportunities to maintain and pass on Korean culture to their American-born children. Throughout the 1920s and 1930s, Hawaii was home to a number of Korean schools for both boys and girls, summer Korean language classes, and other cultural offerings such as traditional dance lessons. Also, the steady influx of Korean-born college students who passed through Hawaii on their way to the mainland allowed Koreans to maintain ties with their homeland in a way that was not possible for Koreans on the West Coast.

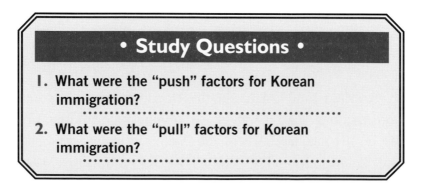

• Study Questions •

1. What were the "push" factors for Korean immigration?

2. What were the "pull" factors for Korean immigration?

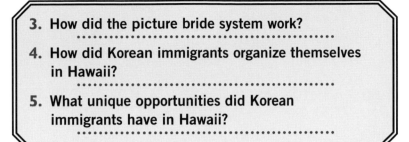

3. How did the picture bride system work?
....

4. How did Korean immigrants organize themselves in Hawaii?
....

5. What unique opportunities did Korean immigrants have in Hawaii?
....

4

Koreans on the Mainland

In the period before 1965, the largest Korean communities in the United States were in Hawaii and Southern California. Korean immigrants on the mainland numbered only 1,200, but in the larger context of Koreans in the United States, their presence on the mainland was extremely influential.

Korean life on the mainland was quite different than life in Hawaii. Not only was the Korean community much smaller (in Hawaii, Asian immigrants were in the majority), but Korean immigrants also found themselves living alongside other Asian groups in that minority.

One Korean man recalled the situation for Koreans in California in the first decade of the twentieth century: "The plight of the Koreans was sad. There isn't much of a story I can tell. Pitiful Koreans. Their history—such a sad history. They didn't know the language [English] they didn't know how to go about finding a job. Poor things. They had to go hither and yonder in

44

search of jobs. . . . I want to cry when I think of the humiliations they confronted."[14]

In the United States, racial discrimination against Asians and discrimination against immigrants in general made life difficult for Koreans. This was especially true in California. The state was the center of anti-Asian political activity, which resulted in the exclusion of Chinese immigrants in 1882. For the first time, a group was banned from immigrating to the United States based on race. This laid the foundation on the West Coast for profound anti-Asian feeling which negatively affected other Asian immigrants, including Koreans.

In describing the experiences of Korean immigrants in the face of anti-Asian discrimination in California, Easurk Emsen Charr, who published an autobiography of his experiences as an immigrant in 1961, recalled,

> Personal insults were offered the Oriental, calling him "Jap," or "Scaby," meaning a scab, a dirty fellow who does the same work for lower wages than do others; missiles were thrown at him in the streets; mob violence threatened, school segregation proposed; services denied him at barber shops and restaurants; segregation in small town theatres; refusal of admission into places of amusements; and various other indignities and discriminatory treatment occurred.[15]

Moreover, this racial hostility at times was violent. Charr continued, "In a Southern California town a year or so later, a house where the first Korean laborers moved into was threatened with mob violence by the labor element of the town, but by the timely assistance rendered by the church people of the town the threatened violence was stopped."[16]

In California, in the early years, Korean immigrants were primarily concentrated in the agricultural industry. Koreans were especially successful in farming, because many had previous farming experience in Korea and in Hawaii. Examples of

Many Korean immigrants who settled in California during the early 1900s worked in the agricultural industry, where they helped harvest crops such as grapes. Pictured here are workers in a vineyard in Southern California.

this success include the Kim brothers, who developed the fuzzless peach, and Kim Chong-nim, who in the 1920s was so successful in rice farming, he became known as the "rice king."

As time passed, Koreans moved into other occupations. As they do today, for a number of reasons, Korean immigrants during this time found self-employment desirable. The racism and discrimination toward Asian immigrants prevented even qualified Korean immigrants from holding professional occupations. In fact, even Korean immigrants with college degrees in the 1920s and 1930s found that the only work they could find was domestic work. As a result, Korean immigrants turned to self-employment or businesses that served the ethnic community. Although this practice is certainly part of Korean-

American communities today, it is important to remember that Korean immigrant entrepreneurship has a long history in the United States.

As they did in Hawaii, Koreans in California maintained tight ethnic bonds through churches, language schools for the second generation, women's clubs, and most important, political organizations that made the cause of Korean independence

LA CHOY

When it comes to Chinese food in the United States, one of the best-known brands is La Choy. For more than 80 years, La Choy has dominated the market for quick and easy Chinese food that can be prepared at home. Surprisingly, La Choy was founded in the 1920s by Ilhan New, a Korean immigrant.

Born in 1885 in what is present-day North Korea, New immigrated to the United States in the first decade of the twentieth century; however, New did not represent the typical Korean immigrant. The majority of Korean migrants at the turn of the century were recruited to work in the sugar plantations of the Hawaiian Islands, but New came as a student. He attended the University of Michigan, where he earned a Bachelor of Arts degree and, by 1919, completed a certificate in business administration.

Using the skills he acquired at the University of Michigan, New and his friend Wallace Smith started La Choy Food Products in 1920 and began to sell canned bean sprouts and soy sauce. La Choy was successful enough that, by the 1930s, New was one of the wealthiest Korean immigrants in the United States. Before World War II, New sold his shares to his partner. Today, La Choy is a division of ConAgra Foods.

With the financial success of La Choy, New was one of the few immigrants who was able to return to Korea and establish a financial base in his homeland. After Korean liberation, New returned to Korea and founded Yuhan Corporation, which is currently one of the country's largest pharmaceutical companies.

their main focus. Although this was true for first-generation immigrants, for the American-born generation, the struggle to fit into American society was a more immediate concern. One second-generation woman recalled, "The independence movement seemed to unite the first generation immigrants."[17]

Their parents were concerned with the Korean independence movement and the daily struggle of earning a living, but second-generation Koreans faced their own difficulties. They had to negotiate two worlds—the world of their parents and of a larger America. As a result, the second generation had to figure out how to live as Korean Americans.

The hardest thing the second generation dealt with was the discrimination they faced on a daily basis, despite the fact that they were American citizens. One Korean American recalled, "When I first went to U.C. [University of California, Berkeley] in 1939, I noticed the discrimination right away. I discovered that the white boys wouldn't speak to me."[18]

As a result, second-generation Koreans of the 1930s and 1940s not only formed close friendships with each other, but they also created their own social world. The first generation actively supported this activity and created opportunities for the second generation to maintain their Korean heritage. For example, first-generation Korean immigrants wanted their children to learn Korean. As a result, many American-born Koreans attended Korean language school. In fact, being able to speak Korean was an important part of the Korean-American identity. One second-generation woman recalled, "By the time I was in second grade, I could read and write Korean even though I couldn't understand everything I read. I don't actually remember learning to read and write, but I think my parents must have initially taught me. . . . I also remember going to Korean school with other Korean children."[19]

Another important issue for the first generation when it came to their children was that of marriage. Particularly, first-generation immigrants wanted their children to marry other

Koreans. This was often difficult, especially on the mainland, because the Korean population was so small. One Korean-American woman recalled,

> First of all, you have to realize that my father was ada-
> mant that I marry a Korean. That was impressed upon me
> when I was in high school. My father heard that I danced
> with a Japanese boy once. He didn't tell me, but he told
> my mother. If she ever marries a Japanese boy—I'm going
> to kill her and then myself. . . . It didn't take long for me
> to see that it wasn't just Japanese boys that were off-limits
> for marriage. If I married anyone who was not Korean,
> he would have reacted just as negatively. I felt that I was
> limited in terms of choices. And there really wasn't much
> interracial mixing until after World War II.[20]

At the same time, like other American teenagers during this time, second-generation Koreans attended school dances, went to the movies, went out for ice cream, and played sports. In general, the second generation did manage to be both Korean and American in a time when it was very difficult to be nonwhite.

For Koreans living in the United States before 1965, World War II was a turning point. It became clear that the American involvement in the war was the best way for Japan to be defeated, and, as a result, for Korea to be liberated. Also, for Koreans, like for other immigrants in the United States, World War II became a moment where they could become "more" American. Koreans sold war bonds, raised victory gardens, volunteered for the Red Cross, and most important, served in the U.S. military. Both second-generation Korean men and women were eager to demonstrate their loyalty to America. One Korean-American man recalled,

> It was 1944, and I could no longer remain a civilian . . .
> earning a fat wage. I enlisted. But getting into the army

was not so easy for me. First, they were doubtful about my age—thirty-eight. Then they saw the scar on my back, a reminder of spinal surgery in 1940 for a slipped lumbar disc. When I insisted that I was physically fit, they asked if I would sign a disability waiver. Of course I did; I would sign anything. My enlistment was approved; I was going to war to kill or be killed.[21]

Japanese Americans were interned (forced to live in camps) for the duration of the war, and in many ways this

---

Notable Individual

SUSAN AHN CUDDY

In 2003, Susan Ahn Cuddy was named the 48th Congressional District's (located in Southern California's Orange County) "Woman of the Year" by the California State Assembly. This award recognized her remarkable achievements, both as a Korean-American woman and as a Californian.

The daughter of Ahn Chang-ho, one of the most famous Korean political leaders of the twentieth century, Susan Ahn Cuddy was born in 1915, in Los Angeles, and was one of the first Koreans born in the United States. Influenced by her father's patriotism for Korea and the United States, Ahn Cuddy decided early on that she could be both Korean and American.

The opportunity to fulfill this desire came to pass during World War II. After she finished college, she attempted to enlist in the navy. For Ahn Cuddy, enlistment represented a way to both serve America and, with the defeat of Japan, contribute to Korean independence. Although the navy initially refused to enlist her, Ahn Cuddy was persistent and became the first Asian-American woman in the navy and the first female gunnery officer to graduate

benefited other Asian immigrant groups. Koreans as well as Chinese found their situations greatly improved. Not only were they the "good" Asians, in contrast to the enemy Japanese, but similar to the majority of Americans, the wartime economy provided new opportunities. One Korean-American woman in San Francisco recalled, "The war was terrible, but it also brought opportunity. With the war, not only did people have more money, but there was a lot more assimilation of people as well as neighborhoods."[22]

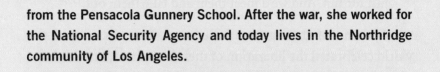

from the Pensacola Gunnery School. After the war, she worked for the National Security Agency and today lives in the Northridge community of Los Angeles.

Susan Ahn Cuddy, pictured here next to an exhibit at the Korean American Museum in Los Angeles on December 5, 2003, is the daughter of renowned Korean political leader Ahn Chang-ho. During World War II, Cuddy enlisted in the U.S. Navy, where she became the first Asian-American woman officer and the first woman gunnery officer.

5

Contemporary Korean Communities in North America

KOREANS IN THE UNITED STATES

Currently, more than one million people of Korean descent live in the United States, with the largest concentration in Southern California and the New York metropolitan area. Korean immigrants have also built significant communities in Chicago and Washington, D.C., and in smaller cites, such as Memphis, Kansas City, and Indianapolis.

The experience of Korean immigrants in the United States can be understood in the two distinctive waves—pre- and post 1965. The Immigration and Naturalization Services Act of 1965, which liberalized American immigration policy to admit Asian immigrants, serves as the chronological dividing line between these two waves of immigration. Between the end of World War II and the changes in American immigration policy in the 1960s, Koreans still continued to enter the United States.

In the 1950s, though, the Korean immigrant population was primarily composed of war brides, the Korean brides of U.S. soldiers, and Korean orphans, who were generally adopted by white American families.

The change in U.S. immigration policy in 1965 allowed for family reunification and the recruitment of professionals, particularly in the medical field, and it revitalized Korean immigration. The new law allowed families to be reunited, because Koreans who had citizenship (this included many of the first-wave immigrants and war brides) were permitted to invite and sponsor immediate relatives (parents, spouses, children) still living in Korea to immigrate to the United States. This situation was the key to mass Korean immigration after 1965. The recruitment of professionals would also have an impact on Korean immigration, especially the recruitment of nurses.

Similar to the Korean immigrants at the turn of the century, post-1965 Korean immigrants faced enormous hardships in the United States as they built a new life for themselves and their families. Although some of these struggles, such as adapting to a new culture and learning a new language, are part of a broader shared immigrant experience, Koreans, along with other non-white immigrants, had to deal with racial discrimination.

The new wave of Korean immigrants turned to self-employment in significant numbers. Koreans as an ethnic group, like previous generations of European immigrants, have come to be associated with specific industries. For example, in New York City, green groceries, nail salons, and corner delis are dominated by Korean immigrants. In California, many Korean immigrants own liquor stores. Also, many run businesses such as restaurants, beauty salons, and travel agencies that serve the ethnic community.

Many Korean immigrants will tell you that the sacrifices they make working in such labor-intensive industries are for their children. Mr. Park, a first-generation Korean immigrant who owns a shoe repair shop declared, "It's going ok. But, gosh,

I didn't know that we would have to work this hard in America. All I do is work, work, work, but it's all right because we can afford three meals a day [in Korean, this expression means he

Korean Immigrants Admitted Under Different Preference Categories, 1998 to 2004

Year	Total	Family-sponsored preferences	Employment-based preferences	Immediate relatives of U.S. citizens (Total)	Spouses of U.S. citizens	Children	Parents
2004	19,766	2,474	8,662	8,602	4,708	2,422	1,472
2003	12,512	1,607	4,297	6,579	3,323	2,252	1,004
2002	21,021	2,164	9,241	9,573	5,315	2,456	1,802
2001	20,742	2,929	8,353	9,420	5,432	2,487	1,501
2000	15,830	3,564	5,580	6,610	3,475	2,149	986
1999	12,840	4,213	3,653	4,914	2,033	2,267	614
1998	14,268	4,336	4,765	5,130	2,417	2,040	673

Source: Department of Homeland Security Web site. Available online at http://www.uscis.gov/graphics/shared/statistics/yearbook/2004/table8.xls

feels financially comfortable], and thank God the kids are doing well in school."[24]

At the same time, after 1965, the gains of the civil rights movement in the United States opened up new opportunities for Asian Americans. As a result, Korean immigrants, and especially their children, have been able to achieve new social mobility in professions such as medicine and law. This is not to suggest that all Korean immigrants have achieved success, however. As for earlier Korean immigrants, many of the same challenges of adapting to a new country, such as language barriers, racial discrimination, domestic violence, and poverty, are still issues of concern.

For post-1965 Korean immigrants, 1992 represented a turning point in these challenges. In April 1992, four white Los

Like many immigrant groups in the United States, Korean Americans have gravitated toward certain industries and jobs. According to one source, as many as 75 percent of Manhattan's green groceries are owned by Korean Americans.

Angeles police officers were declared innocent for the violent beating of Rodney King, a black man. African Americans were rightfully outraged, and three days of civil unrest began. Although hostilities between blacks and whites in Los Angeles had a long history, in 1992, Koreans became caught in the crossfire, as many of their stores were looted and burned to the ground. Korean businesses alone suffered more than $4 million in damages. This was a major financial blow to the Korean community. In addition, the fact that the city of Los Angeles did little to respond in the initial period of crisis suggested to Koreans that, despite their economic success, as a community they were politically and racially isolated.

Due to increased racial tensions caused by the 1992 Los Angeles riots, Korean Americans recognize the importance of developing better relationships with other ethnic groups, especially African Americans. Jae Yul Kim, who had to rebuild after the riots, is pictured here greeting longtime customer McKinley Gipson at his market in South Central Los Angeles.

In the aftermath of the 1992 Los Angeles Riots, Korean immigrants addressed this problem by becoming involved in local politics. They also began to build bridges between Korean communities and other racial groups and worked to promote racial harmony.

Korean immigrant communities are still one of the fastest-growing immigrant groups in the United States. This is due to continued immigration and natural population growth.

KOREANS IN CANADA

Much the same as Korean immigrants in the United States, early Korean immigrants to Canada in the first part of the twentieth century were part of a larger Protestant Christian missionary network. As a result, most were Korean students who came to train as ministers. These Korean students were joined by other students after World War II, and together they established the foundation for the Korean-Canadian community.

Until the 1960s, the number of Koreans remained small and concentrated in Toronto. Changes in Canadian immigration law, however, encouraged mass Korean immigration to Canada. The most recent figures indicate that almost 150,000 Koreans live in Canada, primarily in the Vancouver and Toronto metropolitan areas. Similar to the majority of their counterparts in the United States, Koreans in Canada are recent immigrants and are part of a larger wave of global immigration. Currently, Korea is one of the main sources of Canadian immigrants.[25]

In many ways, the profile of Korean immigrants in Canada is very similar to that of Korean immigrants in the United States. In general, Koreans in Canada have a higher level of education compared to other immigrant groups. They come from urban areas in Korea and many own small businesses. In fact, because they migrated in family units, more than 40 percent of Korean immigrants in Canada work in family businesses, such as convenience stores, video rental shops, fast-food restaurants, and dry cleaners.[26] Given Canada's smaller economy, however,

Korean immigrants as an ethnic group have achieved less economic success than their counterparts in the United States.

For Korean immigrants in Canada, social networks have been important to starting a new life, especially in establishing an economic base. For example, Korean immigrants are often dependent on assistance from earlier waves of immigrants. One Korean immigrant woman said,

> I heard a joke among Koreans here saying, what a new immigrant does upon arriving in Canada depends on the occupation of the person who picks up the immigrant at the airport. That was true! My friend and my husband's friend who came to the airport for us were running convenience stores. Without much consideration, we thought that we should also run a convenience store like them.

As in the United States, Korean women in Canada were more likely to work outside of the home, especially in family-owned businesses. This brought husbands and wives into close working relationships, which was quite different from Korean practice. One woman pointed out, "In Korea, we [my husband and I] were living in completely different worlds."[27]

In contrast, after immigration, Korean men and women found their lives had changed dramatically in terms of working experiences. Some experiences were negative. One woman said, "Yes, of course! As for working together, I see a lot of new things about him, which I didn't know before. . . . Well, I don't think it is a really good thing that a wife and husband work together in the same workplace. I see a lot more bad things than good things about my husband. Naturally, we are more involved in more arguments."[28] For other Korean immigrants, the situation was more positive. One woman stated,

> No, we have never worked together before like this. But, I don't know . . . I heard that a lot of women have some problems with their spouses in the business. We haven't

been like that. Rather, we have quite enjoyed it so far. May-be that is because he was always busy when we were in Korea. We didn't have much time to spend together. Now, we joke around together and work hard together.[29]

Notable Individual

REVEREND SANG-CHUL LEE

Reverend Sang-Chul Lee is one of the most prominent Korean Canadians today.* Born in Siberia in 1924, Lee moved with his family first to Manchuria and then to South Korea, where he converted to Christianity. In 1961, he moved to Vancouver, British Columbia, to pursue his studies. Lonely for his wife and three children, after three years, Reverend Lee returned to Korea and was reunited with his family. His experiences in Canada left him changed, however, and he found it difficult to adjust to life in Korea again.

Fortunately, Reverend Lee was offered a position to serve as a pastor of a Canadian church, which provided the Lee family with the opportunity to immigrate to Vancouver. Lee went on to lead a Korean church in Toronto for more than 20 years. Significantly, Reverend Lee is one of the earliest Korean immigrants, and Canada took his role as a community leader seriously. Not only did he help other Korean immigrants settle in Canada, but he strove to make Canada a truly multicultural society. In 1988, Reverend Lee was appointed a leader of the United Church of Canada, and from 1992 to 1998 he served as the chancellor of Victoria University in Toronto. In 1999, the Korean government presented Reverend Lee with the Korean Overseas Compatriots Prize, in recognition of his contributions to Korean-Canadian society.

* "The Wanderer: The Story of Reverend Sang-Chul Lee." *A Scattering of Seeds: The Creation of Canada.* Available online at *http://www.whitepinepictures.com/seeds/ii/24/index.html.*

The unpaid labor of women has been important to the success of Korean immigrant businesses. At the same time, this often creates an enormous workload for women who now have both domestic and work responsibilities. One Korean immigrant working woman declared, "I do everything. I do the cooking, cleaning, washing dishes and laundry. Sometimes I ask the boys to vacuum. But basically, it is all my work. You see, I live with three men in this house!"[30]

Much like their counterparts in the United States, Korean immigrants in Canada have built thriving ethnic communities, especially in Vancouver and Toronto. Korean communities in these cities include several churches, college alumni associations, business organizations, and businesses that serve Koreans, such as restaurants. For first-generation immigrants, this community structure provides a critical resource for many immigrants who do not speak English or have recently immigrated. It is clear that the Korean population in Canada will continue to grow as a result of both continued immigration and the natural growth of the existing population.

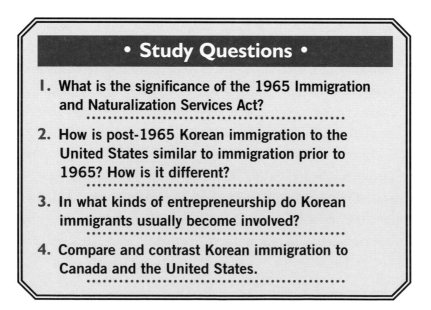

• **Study Questions** •

1. What is the significance of the 1965 Immigration and Naturalization Services Act?

2. How is post-1965 Korean immigration to the United States similar to immigration prior to 1965? How is it different?

3. In what kinds of entrepreneurship do Korean immigrants usually become involved?

4. Compare and contrast Korean immigration to Canada and the United States.

6

Korean Adoptees

In general, when we talk about immigration, we think about individuals making a decision to leave their home country and settle in a new country, such as the United States. This explains how the majority of Korean immigrants came to the United States, but it does not reveal the full story of Korean immigration. An important but understudied aspect of Korean immigration is the adoption of about 200,000 Korean children by American families since the 1950s.

Although domestic adoption has long been a part of the fabric of America, international adoption is a relatively new endeavor. It resulted from the disruptions caused by World War II. In particular, the presence of U.S. soldiers abroad led to personal involvements that produced significant numbers of mixed-raced children. The hostility directed toward and the poor treatment of these children in their home countries shocked Americans.

Before the 1950s, international adoptions, especially of nonwhite children, rarely happened in the United States. This changed in the aftermath of the Korean War (1950–1953), however. In particular, the sad images of Korean war orphans moved the hearts of Americans to adopt these children. At the same time, there was pressure in Korea to encourage the adoption of children of U.S. soldiers and Korean women who were

HOLT INTERNATIONAL

In the 1950s, Bertha and Harry Holt, who lived in Oregon, saw a film about the desperate situation of Korean orphans. Moved by the plight of these orphans, the Holts decided to adopt eight mixed-race Korean children at a time when adopting non-American children was outlawed. In fact, a special presidential order establishing children placement services had to be passed by Congress to permit Americans to adopt Korean children.

As the story of the Holts and their adopted children spread, other American families also expressed their interest in adopting Korean children. Because the Holts already had experience with adoption in Korea, they helped these families, and Holt International was born. Initially, the business was operated out of the kitchen of the Holt home, but Holt quickly became the greatest force behind international adoptions in the United States. Harry Holt died in 1964, but his wife, Bertha, continued the work of Holt International. Although the Holts initially sought to place mixed-race children, today the children from Korea that are placed through Holt International are primarily Korean.

Holt International has placed more than 40,000 Korean children in adoptive homes in the United States. Bertha Holt was so beloved that, until her death in 2000 at the age of 96, she was called "Grandma Holt" by the many children and families she brought together. Currently, Holt International places 1,000 Korean children a year in the United States.

left behind after the war, because Korean society frowned on mixed-race children.

Part of the appeal of Korean adoptions, in comparison with other international adoptions, was that Korean children could be adopted at a very early age—six to eight weeks—unlike children in other countries, who were often older. In addition, the rise of single motherhood in Korea and the demand

During the 1950s, many Americans were touched by the difficult conditions orphans faced in Korea. The children pictured here with their new American parents were adopted through the efforts of Harry and Bertha Holt, who founded Holt International Children's Services in 1955 after they saw a documentary film detailing the plight of children in Korean orphanages.

for infants in the United States continued the demand for Korean children.

The adoption of international children into warm, loving, American homes seems like a good situation for the children and the parents who desperately want them. The issues of racial difference made Korean adoption very difficult at times, however. Most Korean children were adopted into suburban, middle-class, white families in areas of the country without significant Asian communities.

In the earliest period of Korean adoptee migration, the accepted belief was that Korean children should be assimilated into American culture as much as possible. As a result, many of these adoptees knew almost nothing about Korea or Korean culture. As these children became adults, they had many questions about where they were from. Often, many became angry when they were not told about their heritage.

Today, the situation is quite different. American society, in general, has become more accepting of racial differences. In addition, in a multicultural world—one made smaller by the Internet, inexpensive international travel, and globalization in general—parents of Korean adoptees are finding it harder to ignore the racial and cultural differences of their children.

Despite love and care by their families, however, many Korean adoptees experienced racial hostility, especially those Korean children who were adopted into areas of the country that did not have significant Asian populations. One adopted Korean, Janice Bishop, recalled,

> My mom made a point with my family that she wasn't going to tolerate any racist comments. Her attitude was that she had accepted this interracial adoption, and if anyone else wasn't going to, then she wasn't going to have anything to do with them. When I arrived—that was in 1975 or 1976—they did have a lot of problems. They went on a couple of trips back East to visit some of my dad's relatives,

and my mom has memories of driving through Texas and not being served because I was with them.[31]

As for the maintenance of Korean identity, although many white American parents made an effort to teach their adopted children about Korean culture, many adopted Koreans knew nothing about their heritage. Janice Bishop, who had participated in a special trip to Korea for adoptees, said,

> My parents have tried to instill a sense of who I was, but it was kind of hard because they don't have any knowledge of Korean culture. . . . But I came [to the United States] at such a young age that I basically lost all my Koreaness. [My mom] tried to buy me books. She even bought me Korean Barbie doll clothes, and she'd sew pillows with the Korean flag on it. She tried, but I don't think all parents do. A lot of kids had no exposure to Korea at all. Some of them came from Midwest towns where guys didn't want to date them. They never met other Asians. Those were the ones who rejected the Korean culture that we were being exposed to. They didn't like the food and were closed-minded to a lot of things.[32]

As a group, Korean adoptees are well organized. Today, there are many organizations that provide emotional and practical support for adoptees and their families. The Internet has been an essential resource; adoptees have many online resources and have been able to connect with other Korean adoptees throughout the world. As a result of these efforts, older adoptees today have consciously reached out to younger adoptees to offer advice and to serve as a resource.

For many years, Korea was one of the largest sources of foreign adoptions, even as Korea's economy and standard of living improved dramatically. The continued taboos against adoption by Koreans, combined with the economic crisis of the 1990s in Asia, however, continued to make overseas adoption necessary.

Today, American families adopting Korean children rec- ognize the importance of maintaining ties to Korea and Ko- rean culture and to other Korean adoptees. As a result, parents have taken an active role in having their children attend Korean culture camps, travel to Korea, and to attend Korean language school and in general to adopt Korean culture as a family.

At the same time, as Korean adoptees and their families have recognized the importance of maintaining ties to Korea, in the 1990s, the Korean government developed an interest in Korean adoptees. The stories of these adoptees, largely unknown in Ko- rea until recently, captured the hearts of Koreans. One outcome of this interest was "homecoming" visits sponsored by the Ko- rean government and other organizations.

These visits were arranged to provide adoptees with some sense of their heritage. They also served as an opportunity

American families who adopt Korean children recognize the importance of exposing their children to Korean culture. Pictured here is a group of Korean-American adoptees playing *mook chee bah*, a Korean variation of rock, paper, scissors, at the Holt Heritage Camp in New Jersey.

for Korea to include adoptees as part of a larger group of Koreans who lived overseas. For many adoptees, these visits to Korea were incredibly important and answered some of the questions they had about themselves, but not at the expense of their experiences as adoptees. Janice Bishop pointed out,

> The majority of us couldn't find any information about our backgrounds, because most of us had been abandoned. . . . I always wonder what my children are going to look like, and what my biological parents look like, but I don't think that finding my biological parents would fill a void in me, because I have received all the parental nurturing that I need. . . . But now I've reached an age when I could have a child myself, and I understand more what it means for a woman to give up her child. It would be a very hard decision for me. So now, when I think about the things my mom told me about being a healthy baby, I feel a little better about myself, that maybe I wasn't strictly unwanted and abandoned. It's something nice to keep in the back of your head.[33]

In Korea, some of the most dramatic, and most popular, stories of Korean adoptees have been about adoptee–birth parent reunions. Suzanne Switzer, a 15-year-old adoptee, described her feelings,

> I feel like now I know where I came from and know more about me. To me, that is really important. Now I can tell somebody that asks me where I'm from, where I am really from. I feel so much more comfortable about my past now because I know what really happened and I feel more secure with myself. I wait for the next time I will see them because they have grown to be a very important part of my life and I will never think any less of them. I used to think badly of my birthmother and wonder why she gave

me up. Now I know the truth and I just want to thank her for what she did.[34]

As Korean adoptees attempt to come to terms with their experiences, it is clear that a distinct Korean adoptee identity has emerged. For many adoptees, this is an identity, like the identity of Korean-American immigrants, but it is one that is distinct from both American and Korean culture. Despite the fact that Korean adoptees are scattered throughout the world, they have been able to share their common identities and experiences thanks largely to the Internet. Mirim Kim, an adoptee, said,

> In so many ways, I have been blessed. But is that lucky? Is it lucky to be a permanent nomad, always between two cultures? Some people say that all U.S. immigrants face the same dilemma, but I disagree. People who immigrate to the U.S. by choice have family, history and roots somewhere. Adoptees do not. Caucasian immigrants in particular can assimilate racially into mainstream American society. Korean adoptees cannot. Korea is no longer my country, but to some extent neither is the U.S.[35]

For older adoptees, this identity includes a complete denial of their Korean heritage, a sense of isolation due to growing up in all-white communities, and racial discrimination. At the same time, when these adoptees have the chance to return to Korea, they find that there is pressure to be "Korean." Although younger adoptees have had an easier time of being adopted in comparison with older adoptees, adoptees as a whole share a set of experiences that define them. These experiences include being adopted at a very early age, being adopted primarily into white families, limited knowledge about Korea and Korean culture, dealing with racial discrimination, lack of knowledge about their birth families and medical histories, and often the feelings of being rejected by Korean society.

The issue of Korean adoption and international adoption in general still generates many questions about how Korean adoptees should be raised and how their ties to Korea should be maintained. One adoptee's mother put it this way,

> Our main goal was to have a family. I see us less as an adoptive family but a multicultural family. I began to think about what it would be like if we [were] an immigrant Korean family. I make sure that my children are connected to the Korean American community. I've made an effort to make Korean friends and get involved in Korean American organizations. From the moment they are placed in your arms, there is an incredible awareness that you are now connected through this tiny baby to an entire family in Korea—birth father, birth mother, siblings, aunts and uncles—an enormous connection. It instantly makes you Korean in your heart.[36]

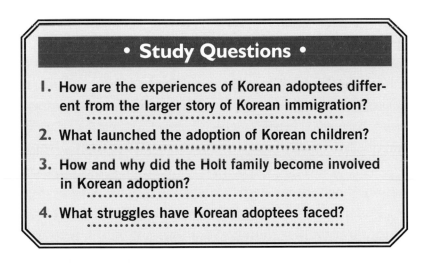

• Study Questions •

1. How are the experiences of Korean adoptees different from the larger story of Korean immigration?

2. What launched the adoption of Korean children?

3. How and why did the Holt family become involved in Korean adoption?

4. What struggles have Korean adoptees faced?

7

Los Angeles, 1992

Days after the Los Angeles riots had officially ended on May 4, 1992, the smell of smoke lingered in the air, and the nation was in a state of shock. More than 50 people had been killed, nearly 2,000 had been injured, more than $1 billion in damage was done, more than 10,000 people had been arrested, and parts of the city had been completely burned to the ground. What had happened in Los Angeles? How could Koreans recover from *sa-i-gu*, which in Korean literally means "April 29," the first day of the riots?

Riots and urban uprisings have occurred in the United States throughout its history. Most uprisings in the twentieth century, especially in the 1960s, were rooted in black/white conflict. What made the riots of 1992 unique, however, was that they were the first multiracial riots involving whites, African Americans, Asians, and Latinos.

By the 1990s, the impact of post-1965 Korean immigration could be seen in cities across the United States. In places like

Chicago, New York, and Los Angeles, the size of Korean populations were significant enough to support visible "Koreatowns."
Many Korean immigrants had become economically successful
by opening their own businesses in poor Latino and African-
American neighborhoods, which often led to conflict. Cultural
misunderstandings also contributed to this situation.

UNDERSTANDING 1992

The Los Angeles riots began on April 29, 1992, in response
to the verdict in the Rodney King trial, where four white police officers were found innocent of the brutal videotaped
beating of King, who was African American. People were
shocked at the verdict, especially in light of the videotaped
evidence. It was especially shocking for African Americans
in Los Angeles.

Anger at the verdict simmered, and soon rioting began in
South Central Los Angeles and spread across the city. Author-
ities did little to stop the rioting and looting, because it was
occurring in predominately nonwhite neighborhoods. Almost
three days of violence and destruction would occur before federal troops were called in to restore order. This pushed many
Korean immigrants to arm themselves to protect their stores.
One Korean immigrant man recalled,

> My wife and I together work twenty-three hours a day,
> seven days a week. There are no days off. I figure that our
> hourly wage is less than minimum wage. Even if I died
> right at this moment, I have nothing to leave behind. . . .
> After the Rodney King verdict, the other stores around
> here were broken into. The windows were smashed. One
> market down the street was completely looted of every-
> thing of value. People broke down my door and started
> looting until I showed them I had a gun. . . . So I shot one
> round in the air. They threw down what they had and left.
> The police didn't even get here until much later.[37]

Images of Korean storeowners shooting guns to ward off looters were shown repeatedly by the media. This made the situation even worse. It made Koreans appear as if they cared more about their property than human life. The bulk of the media coverage failed to address the fact that the police and fire department did little to protect Koreatown. Also, the media failed to recognize that, for many Korean immigrants, these businesses represented a lifetime of work. In the aftermath of the riots, Korean activists were very critical of the biased reporting of the media.

It is important to remember, however, that the Rodney King verdict was part of larger issues in Los Angeles. These included

Images such as this one, in which two Korean-American men protect their store from looters, were repeatedly shown during the media's coverage of the 1992 Los Angeles riots. Unfortunately, Koreatown was not protected by the Los Angeles Police Department, so many Korean Americans were forced to ward off looters.

the high unemployment rate of African Americans and Latinos and a long history of brutality on the part of the Los Angeles Police Department toward African Americans and nonwhites in general. The King verdict also came on the heels of the Latasha Harlins case, where a Korean shopkeeper shot a 15-year-

LATASHA HARLINS AND THE 1992 LOS ANGELES RIOTS

One of the events that contributed to the 1992 Los Angeles riots was the Latasha Harlins case. Harlins, a 15-year-old black girl, was shot to death by Soon Ja Du, a convenience store owner, in an African-American neighborhood in South Central Los Angeles in March 1991. A videotape from a security camera revealed that Du and Harlins quarreled over a container of orange juice that Harlins had put in her backpack without paying for it. It quickly turned into a physical exchange of blows. As Harlins turned away, Du shot her in the back. The African-American community was in disbelief when Du was sentenced to community service, a $500 fine, and probation for the death of Harlins. Although it is difficult to fully understand the leniency of the sentence, it is clear that African Americans were outraged and considered the Harlins case to be part of a larger pattern of discrimination and injustice against African Americans.

Activists responded by organizing a series of boycotts against Korean-owned stores. A number of people pointed to the Harlins incident as a critical event in the days preceding the 1992 uprisings. Walter Thompson, an African-American man, put it this way, "We're mad for a whole lot of reasons. First that 15-year-old girl was killed and they got away with it. Then they beat Rodney King like a dog and the jury sets them free. The black people don't get no justice, nowhere, no time."*

* Don Terry, "Decades of Rage Created Crucible of Violence," *New York Times*, May 3, 1992.

old African-American girl to death during an altercation over a carton of juice.

There were other racial tensions, as well. Like other cities, Los Angeles had experienced an influx of new immigrants, primarily from Asia and Latin America. As a result, Latino immigrants began to move into historically African-American neighborhoods, and Korean immigrants dominated the retail trade in these neighborhoods.

KOREAN IMMIGRANT ENTREPRENEURS

Korean business owners entered African-American neighborhoods because of a particular set of events. In Los Angeles, the race riots of the 1960s had left African-American communities without many necessary services. This allowed Korean immigrants to open businesses such as liquor stores, convenience stores, small grocery stores, wig stores, and nail salons there in the 1970s and 1980s. Koreans were also able to open and maintain these businesses, because they brought savings from Korea and depended on unpaid family labor. At the same time, despite the desires of African Americans, racial discrimination prevented many of them from operating businesses in their own neighborhoods. For example, because of discriminatory lending practices, many blacks could not secure loans to start businesses or to purchase real estate.

The influx of Korean-owned businesses and Latino immigrants into African-American neighborhoods brought the new immigrants and African Americans into close contact. At times, this proximity was marked by cultural misunderstandings and racial discrimination by all parties involved. It is also important to recognize that, for Korean immigrants, there was a cost attached to doing business in poor neighborhoods. One Korean immigrant described it as a war zone:

> I know that many Korean store owners have been killed.
> I feel like this is a war zone and that my life has become

like a battle. If I close my eyes or relax my vigilance for a second, I might lose my life. . . . I am scared every day. I have been beaten, cursed, spat upon. Sometimes young kids demand cigarettes, and if I don't sell to them, they get angry. Once someone threw a bottle at me. If I hadn't blocked it with my arm, I would have been hit in the face. The bottle broke on contact, and I had to go get stitches in my arm.[38]

It would be a mistake to characterize all African-American/Korean encounters as negative, however. One researcher's study of the relationship between blacks and Koreans points out that it is possible to have a relationship of mutual respect:

> Mr. B. is a thirty-year-old Korean male who has operated a liquor store for six years in Southwest Los Angeles. . . . What is interesting about this Korean owner is that for the six years that he has been in business at the present location, he has employed all African Americans and these employees actually run the business in Mr. B's frequent absences. During the riots, Mr. B's business was guarded by the employees and neighborhood people. Mr. B services over 90 percent African Americans. When asked why he has always employed African Americans, Mr. B. stated, "Nearly 100 percent of our customers are African Americans. It would be a slap in the face to the people who live in this community if I did not hire African Americans. And it's good for business."[39]

AFTERMATH

As order was restored, the toll of the rioting was shocking. More than 50 people were killed, 2,000 injured, and 10,000 arrested. Property damage totaled more than $1 billion. At least 2,000 Korean immigrant businesses were burned to the ground, and the Korean community alone sustained more than $4 billion in damages.

Korean immigrant communities across the United States were shocked and angry after the Los Angeles riots, and many wondered if immigrating had been a good decision. In fact, many Korean immigrants left Los Angeles and moved to other parts of the United States. Others tried to figure out how and why Koreans were the target of such violence. One Korean immigrant woman, who watched her store burn down, said,

> Until last year I believed America is the best. I still believe it. I don't deny that now because I'm a victim, but as the year ends in '92 we were still in turmoil and having all the financial problems and mental problems. Then a couple of months ago I realized that Korean immigrants were left out from this society and we were nothing. What is our right? Is it because we are Korean? Is it because we have no politicians? Is it because we don't speak good English? Why? Why do we have to be left out?[40]

Many Koreans who lost their businesses during the riots believed that the looting and burning of Korean businesses was not about African-American hostility toward Koreans but about misplaced anger toward whites and the long history of discrimination against African Americans. One Korean remarked:

> I respect African Americans, their effort in history up to now, how they fought to settle down in this country. They are a model for many minorities living in this country. There were so many great black leaders, like Martin Luther King and others. I am trying to study them. King was a role model for all of us. . . . To me, it wasn't right for the African Americans, who have accumulated their anger and resentment against white people to take it out on the Koreans at this time.[41]

In addition, many Korean immigrants recognized that a larger structure of urban poverty and lack of political power also contributed to the uprising.

One important consequence of the 1992 Los Angeles riots was the entry of Korean Americans into mainstream American politics and the rise of Korean-American political activism. This was important not just for Koreans but for African Americans and Latinos, too. The riots marked a major turning point for Korean immigrant communities. Korean immigrants saw that they could no longer live isolated from mainstream American society. At the same time, many second-generation Korean Americans realized that, to protect the hard work of their parents and their own place in American society, they would have to become politically involved.

In the years immediately after the riots, a new generation of political leaders emerged. These leaders include Angela Oh, an attorney, who became the spokesperson for the Korean community in Los Angeles after the riots. In 1997, Oh was appointed to President Clinton's Initiative on Race. In 1992, California Republican Jay Kim became the first Korean American elected to Congress. Korean Americans also registered to vote in record numbers and began to actively participate in the Democratic and Republican parties.

Today, many Koreans understand the limits of the ethnic community in a multiracial society and are working to build alliances with other racial and ethnic groups. One Korean-American activist put it this way:

> At the time of the riots, African American communities were politically strong, but economically frustrated, Asian American communities were economically stronger and politically invisible, and Latino communities were both politically and economically disenfranchised. Ultimately, we need a multiracial coalition that supports true equality and enfranchisement. The toughest part will be convincing

Attorney Angela Oh emerged as a spokesperson for the Korean-American community after the 1992 Los Angeles riots. In 1997, Oh was one of seven prominent civic figures appointed by former President Bill Clinton to serve on the Presidential Advisory Board on Race Relations, which was established to improve race relations in the United States. Oh is pictured here with fellow board members Thomas Kean (left) and John Hope Franklin during the board's first meeting in July 1997.

those with the most that even if a redistribution of power means no gains for them in the short term, the society as a whole will be better for everyone in the long term.[42]

Today, although many of the issues of race and class are unresolved, the lessons of 1992 have not been forgotten. People of all racial backgrounds understand that it will take a genuine multicultural alliance to avoid racial tensions that could potentially escalate into another armed conflict.

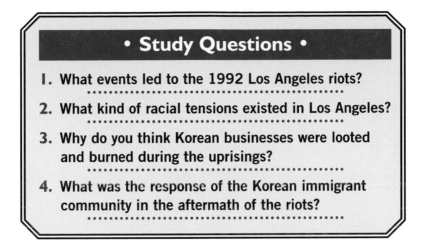

• Study Questions •

1. What events led to the 1992 Los Angeles riots?

2. What kind of racial tensions existed in Los Angeles?

3. Why do you think Korean businesses were looted and burned during the uprisings?

4. What was the response of the Korean immigrant community in the aftermath of the riots?

8

Achievements and Challenges for Korean Immigrants

ACHIEVEMENTS

In the context of post-1965 immigration from Latin America and Asia, Korean immigrants have been very successful. Like earlier newcomers from Asia and Europe, Koreans have established significant communities in urban areas, primarily in Southern California and in New York.

In a fairly short period of time, Koreans have established visible Koreatowns, most notably in New York and Los Angeles but also in smaller cities. Koreatowns have proved important because they provided Korean immigrants with a number of resources. For new Korean Americans, a thriving ethnic community provides a job, a place to live, and in general, critical information about how to settle in the United States. At the same time, Koreatowns provide important ways for immigrants to maintain ties to their homeland. For example, Koreatowns offer

States with the Highest Population of Korean Americans, 2000	
State	**Korean-American Population**
California	345,882
New York	119,846
New Jersey	65,349
Illinois	51,453
Washington	46,880

Source: 2000 U.S. census

Korean restaurants and grocery stores, Korean bookstores and movie theatres, and other cultural attractions.

The economic success of Korean entrepreneurs in the United States is one of the community's most significant achievements. Today, Korean immigrants as a group have the highest rate of self-employment. In many ways, the visibility of Koreatowns represents the economic success of Korean immigrants. The large number of Korean immigrants have allowed other Korean immigrants in the area to open businesses that serve their fellow immigrants. These businesses include restaurants, travel agencies, grocery stores, hair salons, and so on.

At the same time, Korean immigrant entrepreneurs have made their mark beyond Koreatown. In a short period of time, Korean immigrants have come to dominate a number of industries, including green groceries, nail salons, delis, liquor stores, wig stores, and convenience stores. Significantly, Korean immigrants have established such businesses in primarily African-American neighborhoods.

One reason that Korean immigrants have been able to succeed economically is because of their class backgrounds. Unlike previous waves of immigrants to the United States,

Korean grocery stores, such as this one in Wheaton, Maryland, offer Korean food products to Korean Americans and non-Korean Americans alike. According to the 2000 U.S. census, there were approximately 1.3 million Korean Americans living in the United States, including more than 39,000 in Maryland.

Koreans are unique in that a significant number of them came from middle-class backgrounds and have college degrees. They also came with money to invest. At the same time, a strong ethnic community provided additional resources. The personal sacrifices that Korean immigrant families were willing to make also contributed to the success of their businesses. One prosperous Korean businessman described his experiences running a small market:

> We operated that store from 8:00 A.M. to 8:00 P.M., seven days a week, three hundred sixty-five days a year. We would get up every day at 5:00 A.M., pick up the produce from the Central Wholesale Market, stop off at a wholesale

general merchandise market to pick up cigarettes and sundries, and then open up the store. The only vacation we ever had was on December 28, 1988, when we sold the Western market, and March 1, 1989, when we started the Manchester store. That was the only time off we ever had, between October 1, 1984, and April 29, 1992, when the Los Angeles riots disrupted everything. . . . We ran the store by ourselves—my wife, my children, and me. That's how we were able to minimize our expenses.[43]

Another important achievement of Korean immigrants has been their ability to maintain a strong cultural identity and a tight-knit community. For Korean immigrants, one of the most important institutions for the maintenance of ethnic identity has been the Korean church. Like the earliest Korean immigrants, the majority of Korean immigrants today identify themselves as Christians and belong to Korean ethnic churches.

For many Korean immigrants, the church represents more than a place to worship. Korean churches have served as the "glue" for the immigrant community. They provide social services for new immigrants, including English language courses and citizenship classes. At the same time, the ethnic church emerged as one of the most important forces in teaching and maintaining Korean culture for the American-born generation. Many Korean churches also provide instruction in traditional dance and music. These types of cultural offerings were particularly important to Korean immigrants who lived outside areas with significant Korean populations. As many researchers have pointed out, no matter where Korean immigrants settle, one of first things they do is establish a church.

In addition to entrepreneurship and the maintenance of a strong ethnic identity, Korean immigrant communities have been praised for the second generation's educational achievements and the sacrifices of the first generation that made this possible. As a result, significant numbers of Korean Americans attend elite colleges such as Harvard, Yale, and the University of California, Berkeley. In general, compared to other ethnic and racial groups, Koreans have one of the highest rates of college attendance.

CHALLENGES

The story of Korean immigration to the United States is not just a story of achievement, however. Like other immigrant communities, hardship and struggle is also part of this story. Examining the challenges of Korean immigrant communities reveals the impact of post-1965 immigration.

KOREAN NAIL SALONS

In the 1980s, Korean immigrant women pioneered the nail-care industry in the United States. At a time when manicures were limited to the very wealthy or were done at home, the influx of Korean female entrepreneurs changed all this, and soon manicures were widely available at reasonable prices.

Korean-owned nail salons are unique for a number of reasons. First, within Korean immigrant communities, it is an industry dominated by women. In places like New York, Korean women operate roughly 2,000, or 70 percent, of the city's nail salons.* It is understandable why Korean immigrant women become involved in the nail salon industry. Getting a license requires less than a year of training, and many beauty schools cater to Korean immigrant women. In addition, it is work that requires minimal English language skills, and the demand for manicurists is high. It also pays well in comparison to other kinds of work. On average, a manicurist can earn $100 a day before tips. Also, for owners, the start-up costs are low.

Currently, Ji Baek is one of the most successful Korean immigrant nail salon owners. She is the owner of the Rescue Beauty salons in New York and has her own line of nail polishes.

"New" Korean Immigrants

Although middle-class and upper-class professionals made up the earliest wave of post-1965 immigration, in the 1980s and 1990s, working-class Koreans also began to immigrate to the United States. In contrast, these immigrants were less educated, had less money, and had fewer opportunities for social mobility. Instead of owning businesses or pursuing professional careers, these immigrants generally work for other Koreans as cashiers, waitresses, janitors, and so on. Without education and money, working-class immigrants have little to offer except their labor,

Articles about her cutting-edge nail fashions have appeared in such magazines as *Vogue,* and she has served as a consultant for numerous fashion shows.

Immigrating to the United States at the age of 12, Baek trained as a classical musician until an injury ended her career. At first, her parents were against the idea of their daughter operating a nail salon. Baek recalls, "When I told my mom I was going to open a nail salon, she fainted. I am Korean, so it was just so stereotypical—85 percent of the nail salons in New York City are Korean owned. My parents feared I was throwing away the opportunities this country can offer."**

Baek's luxurious chain of nail salons redefined the industry that had brought manicures to the masses. She focused not only on unique nail treatments and designs, she also made sure that the salon itself was a relaxing space. Today, Baek owns three Rescue Beauty salons and is a leader in the industry.

---

* Miliann Kang, "The Managed Hand: The Commercialization of Bodies and Emotions in Korean Immigrant-owned Nail Salons," *Gender and Society* 17, no 6: p. 824.

** Cora Daniels, "Ji Baek Rescue Salons," CNN Money.com (December 1, 2003).

KYES: ROTATING CREDIT ASSOCIATIONS

Korean immigrants have been very successful in starting their own businesses for a number of reasons. One critical component of opening a business is start-up funding. It is very difficult for recent immigrants to borrow money from a bank, however, because they have no credit history and have been in the United States only a short time. Instead, Korean immigrants have brought to the United States the Korean practice of *kye*, or a rotating credit association. A kye operates as follows: For example, if 12 families belong to a kye, each family contributes $1,000 every month. Each family would get one month's worth of kye money; in this example, each family would have access to $12,000 once a year. This pooling of financial resources provides many Korean immigrants with the initial money to start a business. More important, not only do kyes provide financial resources, they also encourage immigrants to organize and build a political foundation. Rotating credit associations are not unique to Korean immigrant communities; many immigrant groups have used such means to establish themselves financially in the United States.

and, as a result, many work more than one job to make ends meet. The success of earlier Korean immigrants, however, has overshadowed the poverty and problems of working-class Koreans, as well as problems within Korean immigrant communities. One Korean immigrant put it this way:

> Many people think that all Koreans go to Harvard and [get] A-pluses, that all Koreans are rich. This is not so. This community has a lot of tragedies, a lot of stereotyping in reverse. We have a lot of poor and uneducated people. Their living conditions are terrible, one crowded room, everyone working two or three jobs, without life insurance, dental or medical benefits, pensions, workmen's compensation.[44]

Downward Mobility

Despite their achievements, Koreans have problems and issues that all immigrant groups have had to deal with. These

Many Korean churches, such as Saint Agnes Catholic Church in
Los Angeles, have dance troupes that perform traditional Korean
dances. Pictured here is Yu Sukyung, leading her dance troupe at the
Encuentro 2000 conference at the Los Angeles Convention Center.

challenges include learning English, looking for work, and in general adapting to American society. Even middle- and upper-class Koreans faced these challenges. Many Korean immigrants who were part of the professional class in Korea experienced downward mobility in the United States. For example, one second-generation Korean American described the adjustments his family had to make in the United States. In Korea, his father was a mechanical engineer and his mother came from a wealthy background. In the United States, his parents worked a wide range of low-wage jobs, until they saved enough money to go into business for themselves. He says:

> When my parents immigrated to America, my father became a mechanic and my mother started working as a motel room cleaner. . . . Just as I was starting seventh grade, my parents started a sidewalk stand in the District of Columbia. They sold handbags and fake gold rings. . . . They have always made it clear that this is privileged information, but I am proud of our humble beginnings in America.[45]

The Cost of Success

Although the high rates of Korean immigrant self-employment have been celebrated as a success, there has also been a cost for this success. One Korean American commented, "Take the typical Korean family. Materially, they may be well off, but in every other way, they are living in poverty. They absolutely have no life except working."[46]

The amount of time that Korean immigrants devoted to their businesses has had a cost, especially for the children, in terms of family relationships:

> I spent most of my weekends working and playing at the store. . . . After the stores opened, we never took another family vacation. I used to feel so resentful. Since

my parents worked eighty hours a week, I rarely really saw them, even if we were at the store together. I learned to be independent and became more and more distant from my parents, the culture and language gap became insurmountable.[47]

In addition, for recent Korean immigrant families, children act as translators, which is demanding and also reverses the child-parent roles. One Korean-American girl stated:

I came five years ago. I live with my parents. They're working and can't speak English well, so at the store, if something happens, I have to help them. They can't do anything. I have to help them with bills. If something goes wrong with the license I have to go to city hall, even though I don't know what to do and I have to deal with adults and I'm just a young person and I don't really know what to do. I would like to just be a student and have a home life, but I have to solve my parents' problems too.[48]

For other Korean Americans, their parents' expectations also produce high levels of stress. Many Korean Americans feel obligated to pursue "safe" careers and fulfill the desires of their parents, especially as they see firsthand the sacrifices their parents have made. One Korean American said,

Parents come here for their children's future, so they want you to do certain things, and you hear it all the time. If I find something that I really like to do and my parents don't approve, there's more distance. Now my parents have given up—now they want me to do what I want. But for a while, that was the hardest thing—fighting with my parents about what I wanted to do. . . . There was pressure to do well, not a fierce pressure, but just guilt because your parents are working 7 days a week. So I was all primed to become a doctor and I got into medical school.[49]

For Korean Americans, the pressure of the *model minority* also has had a negative impact in the pressure it creates. One Korean-American student who was not particularly good in math recalled, "I had this math teacher in high school. I was really bad in geometry, and one time I got a B on a test and she called me aside, and she wanted to know if I had studied and I said I wasn't good in geometry and she said that I should be good at it. I guess it's good if they think you're smart but they shouldn't expect that just because you're Asian."[50]

Problems Within Korean Communities

Korean communities also have a darker side. Domestic violence is a serious problem in Korean immigrant communities. In fact, among Asian Americans, Koreans have the highest rate of domestic violence against women.[51] One Korean immigrant was repeatedly beaten by her abusive husband:

> The beatings started the day they returned from their honeymoon. He choked her until his hands made purple impressions on her throat, she said. He punched and kicked her, and slammed her head against the car door, sometimes smiling all the while. . . . She told herself: "This is my life. I must tolerate it. Even his mom and dad were aware of the abuse. . . . They said, 'Endure it, endure it, you need to just swallow it. You don't know what goes on in the United States. You don't know anything.'"[52]

Although domestic violence is a problem that affects all of American society, immigrant women are especially at risk, because they often cannot speak English, are isolated because they work in family businesses, and do not know about the resources for victims of abuse.

Domestic violence is also part of a larger pattern of family violence. One Korean-American woman described her father's behavior:

There were lots of episodes where he would be very un-happy about something. I'm sure it had to do with the business not being good. He would feel frustrated and come home. We'd all be sitting around at the table and he would pick a fight about something. . . . He would sweep everything off the table. All the dishes would break. For a long time, we didn't have a complete set of dishes. We were always replacing them. He used to throw ashtrays and glasses.

MODEL MINORITY

The term *model minority* first surfaced in the media in the 1960s to refer to the successes of Asian immigrant com-munities in contrast to other minority groups, such as Latinos and African Americans. These successes include low of levels of crime, a high number of college graduates, and higher incomes. There was a political reason why the "model minority" thesis emerged during this period. It was used to critique the poverty and lack of social mobility within Latino and African-American communities. It asked, if Asian immigrants could "make it" by their own efforts in American society, why couldn't other minor-ity groups?

The "model minority" thesis poses a number of prob-lems. This interpretation ignores the long history of racism and discrimination in the United States. At the same time, the "model minority" thesis assumes that all Asians are suc-cessful, which ignores the fact that problems also exist for Asian immigrant communities. It is true that many Asian im-migrants are successful, but many are not. For example, it ignores the desperate poverty and social problems of many re-cent Asian immigrants. The emphasis on success also ignores the very real effects of racial discrimination experienced by Asian Americans.

Oftentimes, children would come between their parents,

> I think I was about six or seven. I could hear my parents arguing in the kitchen, and of course my sister and I were out in the front yard. Then, I don't know why, but I must have run in and said "stop" or something. He hit me. . . . When he hit me, I flew across the kitchen. I don't remember the pain, only being stunned and blacking out for a second. Then my mother came and said, "Don't come in; don't interfere. I don't want you to get hurt."[53]

Criminal activity by Korean youth is another serious problem within Korean immigrant communities. In places like Los Angeles and New York, gang activity is an issue. Korean youth often involve themselves in gangs in response to the presence of other ethnic gangs. Sometimes involvement is a response to the poverty in which many Korean immigrants are raised. One Korean gang member said,

> I'm trying to get out of the gang, but every time I look at this burn on my hand from getting jumped in [initiated], it reminds me that I'm always going to be in this gang because it's going to be for life, unless I get laser surgery or something. If I hadn't gotten this burn I could get out faster. There are certain ways to get out. It takes a long time. You don't want to get jumped out. If they jump you out, they're just going to beat up on you every time they see you again, like at the store or at a party. I'm going the way where they just forget about you. I want to gradually fade out.[54]

Korean immigrants face problems within their communities, but they also face challenges as a minority group in the United States. Racial discrimination has been especially painful for second-generation Korean Americans. One Korean American explains: "As a child you are sensitive; you don't want to be different. You want to be like other kids. I was made to understand that I was different, and the differences were negative.

They made fun of my face. They called me 'flat face.' When I got older, they called me 'chink' or 'jap' or said 'remember Pearl Harbor.' In all cases it made me feel terrible."[55]

Korean immigrants, especially those living in urban areas, have also had to negotiate relationships with other non-white groups. As a result, Korean immigrant communities found that they needed to deal with their own prejudices and discrimination toward African Americans, Latinos, and also, working class Koreans. One Korean-American community activist put it this way:

> People of all different races have anti-immigrant feelings.
> Blacks, Latinos, Koreans have them, and certainly European

Korean Americans recognize the importance of creating alliances with other ethnic groups. To that end, civic leaders such as Danny Park (pictured here, center), who is the executive director of the Koreatown Immigrant Workers Alliance in Los Angeles, have worked to build solidarity among ethnic groups and fight for higher wages.

American people have a lot. But because we are all in it together, we have to think about who really gets the most out of the poor—Latinos, Korean immigrants, people of color—fighting each other. We have to direct our anger and frustration toward the right target. Otherwise, we are going to be fighting each other, and that's not going to take anyone toward any solution.[56]

Many Korean immigrants have discovered that, although a strong Korean community is important and useful, it is also necessary to build political and personal alliances with non-Koreans.

Affirmative Action

Korean immigrants have suffered because of racial discrimination, but they have also benefited to some degree from being an underrepresented minority in the United States. Like women, Native Americans, African Americans, and Latinos, Asian Americans have gained from U.S. *affirmative action* policies. Dating to the 1960s, affirmative action was developed by the U.S. government to address the inequality experienced by various groups in employment and higher education. Korean immigrants, like other Asian immigrants, benefited enormously from affirmative action in the 1970s and 1980s. The relative success of Asian immigrants in terms of educational attainment, employment, and income suggests the success of affirmative action for Asian Americans.

This success has also created the perception that Asian immigrants have "made it" and no longer need affirmative action. Although this may be true for some, not all Asian immigrants have achieved educational and occupational success. For example, many recent Korean immigrants come from working-class backgrounds and live in poverty. The experiences of poor Korean immigrants are ignored in the larger context of Asian-American success. Given the high level of achievement for Koreans in the United States as a whole, many Korean Americans are deeply ambivalent about affirmative action. Indeed, although many in the Korean immigrant community have "made it," events such as the 1992 Los Angeles riots and continued racial discrimination against Asian immigrants serve as clear indicators that affirmative action policies are still necessary.

The challenges Korean immigrant communities face are complicated, and there are no easy solutions. Community activists and organizations recognize these problems, however, and have begun to work toward resolving these issues.

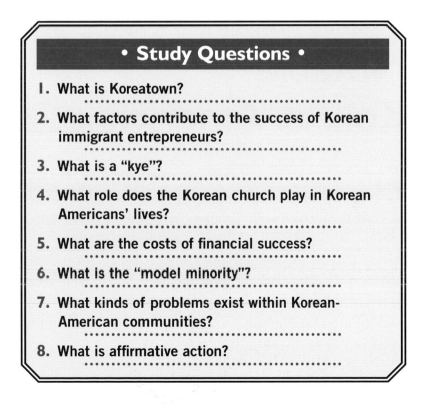

• Study Questions •

1. What is Koreatown?

2. What factors contribute to the success of Korean immigrant entrepreneurs?

3. What is a "kye"?

4. What role does the Korean church play in Korean Americans' lives?

5. What are the costs of financial success?

6. What is the "model minority"?

7. What kinds of problems exist within Korean-American communities?

8. What is affirmative action?

9

Notable Korean Americans

Despite the long history of Korean immigration in the United States, very little is known about the accomplishments of Korean Americans. In the more than 100 years of immigration, Korean Americans have accomplished extraordinary things. There have been novelists, musicians, actors, military leaders, politicians, and Olympic athletes. At the same time, there are the unsung heroes—ordinary people who have made contributions both to Korean-American communities and to American society as a whole.

PHILIP JAISOHN: KOREAN-AMERICAN PIONEER

In the earliest period of Korean immigration, Philip Jaisohn (Soh Chae Pil) was one of the most prominent and well-known Korean Americans. Born in Korea in 1864, his life spanned some of the most significant periods of Korean and American history.

Jaisohn spent his early career as a government official in Korea. He recognized that, for Korea to survive the nineteenth century, there needed to be political change. In an effort to promote this change, Jaisohn was involved in a failed attempt to overthrow the Korean monarchy. With his life at stake, he managed to escape to the United States thanks to his American missionary connections.

Once in the United States, Jaisohn became the first Korean immigrant to receive American citizenship in 1890. Two years later, he became the first Korean-American doctor, after he earned his medical degree at what is now George Washington University, in Washington, D.C. Despite his success in the United States, he retained a fondness for his homeland, and in 1896, he returned to Korea in hopes of modernizing the country.

In Korea, he began a program of reform. He started a newspaper, founded the Independence Club, an organization dedicated to the modernization of Korea, and taught high school. Korea was not ready for such change, however, and in 1898, Jaisohn returned to the United States and settled in Philadelphia.

For Jaisohn, the colonization of his homeland by the Japanese in 1910 was not a surprise. He had recognized Japan's growing power in the nineteenth century and in many ways tried to alert his fellow Koreans about Japan's ambitions. After 1910, Jaisohn devoted his efforts to Korean independence. He not only donated every penny he could afford to the cause, but he worked tirelessly to keep the United States informed about the Korean situation. For this purpose, he established the Korean Information Bureau; published the *Korean Review*, a monthly newsletter; and lectured across the country about Korea. He did all this in addition to practicing medicine.

In his work for the Korean independence movement, Jaisohn was unusual for a number of reasons. At a time when the Korean community in the United States was bitterly

Philip Jaisohn (1864–1951), pictured here speaking before the Korean Liberty Congress in 1942, was the first Korean to become a naturalized U.S. citizen. In addition to being an accomplished physician and businessman, Jaisohn was an advocate for Korean independence from Japanese rule and served as the U.S. Military government's chief advisor during the time of the founding of the Korean Republic in 1948.

divided on how Korea should achieve independence, Jaisohn was respected by the majority of Korean Americans for his dedication to his homeland.

After Korea gained its independence at the end of World War II, Jaisohn returned to his beloved country as an adviser for the U.S. government, until the founding of South Korea in 1948. Jaisohn died in the United States in 1951, at the age of 87. He was truly the first Korean American, who, over the course of his long life, never lost sight of his love and dedication to Korea and his adopted land.

DORA YUM KIM: COMMUNITY LEADER

Born in 1921 in California, Dora Yum Kim was the daughter of Korean immigrants. Her father was a railroad worker and her mother a picture bride. Growing up in San Francisco's Chinatown, as a second-generation Korean American, Kim was a minority within a minority population. The struggles of her immigrant family in an America hostile to Asian immigrants made an important mark on Kim. In the 1960s and 1970s, while working for the state of California, she placed more than 3,000 Korean immigrants in their first jobs.[57] In particular, Kim facilitated the employment of Korean nurses. She recalled making personal sacrifices to help Korean immigrants:

> In order to make space for the programs we were starting for the new immigrants, my son, Tommy, and I started a Korean community center at a storefront on Larkin Street. The nurses' course was already set as a six-month course, so we needed the space for at least that length of time. We relied heavily on donations and volunteers to run the place. My husband, Tom, paid the rent for six months there, my daughter Debby worked at the reception, and that's where I arranged classroom space for the course.[58]

She also cofounded the first Korean community center in the United States and a meal program for Korean senior citizens. When Kim was asked why she had devoted so much time to serving the Korean immigrant community, she responded,

It's certainly rewarding to be appreciated for the things you've done, but I don't think that alone can carry you through. You have to do it because you believe in it. I do things because they need to be done. Whether I can do it, whether I want to do it, or whether I should or shouldn't do it—those questions are irrelevant. If you think too much about doing something, it won't get done. And if you have to think that much about doing something, maybe you shouldn't be doing it. You just have to do what needs to be done, if you know that it is the right thing.[59]

SAMMY LEE: KOREAN-AMERICAN OLYMPIAN

Until recently, the athletic achievements of Asian immigrants have generally been ignored. Although the careers of individuals such as NBA star Yao Ming are well known, it is important to recognize that there is a long history of Asian-American athletes.

In the 1940s and 1950s, one of the most famous swimmers in the United States was Sammy Lee. Born in Fresno, California, in 1920, Lee was the son of Korean immigrants. In 1948, Lee earned the distinction of being the first Asian American to win a gold medal at the Olympics, and in 1952, he was the first man to win back-to-back gold medals in diving.

Lee began diving competitively in high school in Los Angeles. He won numerous awards and graduated as valedictorian of his class. He continued his athletic career at Occidental College, where he became one of the top-ranked divers in the country. After graduating at the top of his class, Lee entered medical school at the University of Southern California and continued to dive.

In addition to the hard work involved in training to be a competitive diver, Lee also faced adversity in the form of discrimination. He recalled, "I would practice at the Los Angeles Swim Stadium and Brookside pool but nonwhites could use the pool only at Brookside one day a week, on Wednesday. And then the pool was emptied after we used it, and fresh water was brought in the next day."[60]

In 1948, Lee won the Olympic gold medal in platform diving, and four years later he won the gold medal again. For Lee, his success at the Olympics represented more than individual achievement: "I wanted to show my fellow Americans that we, Koreans, had a place in American society."[61]

Lee went on to a successful medical career in Los Angeles, and he continued his involvement in the sport of diving by coaching the U.S. Olympic team in 1960. For his achievements and dedication to diving, Lee was inducted into the U.S. Olympic Hall of Fame in 1990 and carried the Olympic torch during the 2004 Olympics in Athens, Greece.

MARGARET CHO: KOREAN-AMERICAN COMEDIAN

Today, Margaret Cho is one of the most recognizable Asian-American Hollywood celebrities. An author, actor, and comedian, Cho has been a pioneer in the industry. Born in San Francisco, Cho is the daughter of the first wave of post-1965 Korean immigrants. Growing up in the vibrant Haight-Ashbury district of San Francisco, Cho became involved in the comedy circuit as a teenager. She won a contest to be the opening act for Jerry Seinfeld and moved to Los Angeles in the 1990s. In Los Angeles, her sharp sense of humor about her experiences as a child of immigrants and as a Korean American kept her in high demand. In 1994, Cho won the American Comedy Award for Best Female Comedian and soon was offered her own television series, *All-American Girl.*

All-American Girl was short lived, and the pressures of Hollywood, especially issues of appearance and race, caused Cho to rethink her acting career. She reflected,

> There were just so many people involved in that show, and so much importance put on the fact that it was an ethnic

Korean-American comedian Margaret Cho became the first Asian-American woman to have a television series based around her when the short-lived *All-American Girl* debuted in 1994. Cho, who is pictured here at her Los Angeles home, also won the American Comedy Award for Best Female Comedian that same year.

show. It's hard to pin down what "ethnic" is without appearing to be racist. And then, for fear of being too "ethnic," it got so watered down for television that by the end, it was completely lacking in the essence of what I am and what I do. I learned a lot, though. It was a good experience as far as finding myself, knowing who I was and what direction I wanted to take with my comedy.[62]

This rethinking led Cho to a series of very successful one-woman shows, including *I'm the One That I Want, Notorious C.H.O., Assassin,* and *Revolution,* which was nominated for a Grammy Award for best comedy album. Cho is also the author of two best-selling books.

For her artistic work and willingness to speak out on matters of social justice, Cho has received numerous awards, from such groups as the National Gay and Lesbian Task Force, the National Organization for Women, and the American Civil Liberties Union (ACLU), who gave her their First Amendment Award. Cho put it this way:

I didn't mean to be a role model. I just speak my truth. I guess speaking from your heart really creates a huge impact, and if I can encourage people to do that, then I would love to be a role model. If I could encourage people to use their voices loudly, then that's my reward. I don't care about winning an academy award; I don't care about mainstream acceptance, because it's never going to be what I want it to be. I just want to do my work and love it.[63]

ANGELA OH: ATTORNEY AND POLITICAL ACTIVIST

In the aftermath of the 1992 Los Angeles riots, Angela Oh, a second-generation Korean-American attorney, emerged as the voice of the Korean community in America. Oh earned her undergraduate degree at the University of California, Los Angeles, and her law degree from the University of California, Davis. She has taught at the University of California, Irvine; she is also an author and a Buddhist priest.

In the days immediately following the uprising, Oh realized that she could not stand by as Korean immigrants were blamed for the riots. She spoke out against the negative media images of Korean immigrants and worked to provide legal assistance to Koreans who had lost their businesses. She mobilized other Korean Americans to also become involved in rebuilding Los Angeles.

In 1997, Oh was appointed to President Clinton's Initiative on Race. Significantly, she was vocal about insisting that America needed a new way to talk about race. For Oh, the 1992 Los Angeles riots made clear the limitations of understanding race as a black or white issue. Instead, she pointed out that post-1965 America was multicultural:

> As I talked to people all around the country, I was impressed over and over again by the number of really decent people out there. There are so many people trying to find a way to make things work. They aren't filled with hate. It's easy, if you don't have opportunities to really know people of different races and nationalities, to be tricked by what you see or others say.[64]

Oh recognized that, although community was important for Korean immigrants, they did not live in isolation. As a result, she encouraged Korean immigrants to build bridges with other racial groups, especially African Americans, and to participate in local and national politics:

> As far as people of color go, as our numbers grow, we will get more influence over the political process. . . . To me the question is: Will we behave like many of the white people who have power now—will we act out of vengeance? Or will we be able to demonstrate

that not only are we competent but that we have the compassion and the stability to exercise power wisely. I look forward to these challenges and am optimistic about the future.[65]

NATALY KIM: AN ORDINARY LIFE

Notable Korean Americans like Philip Jaisohn, Sammy Lee, Margaret Cho, and Angela Oh are important to the Korean community, but the vast majority of Koreans in the United States lead ordinary lives. These people, too, tell powerful stories about their experiences as immigrants.

Born in 1926 in what is now North Korea, Nataly Kim married young, studied nursing, survived the Japanese occupation, and the Korean War. She arrived in the United States at the age of 60. In Korea, her husband abandoned her with three small children and left her in poverty. To support herself and her children, Mrs. Kim learned how to sew.

Eventually, one of her daughters moved to California, and Mrs. Kim soon followed, to help with her daughter's children. She recalled, "Taking care of my grandchildren was very hard. They were four, six, and nine years old when I first came. I had to take my four-year-old grandson to kindergarten by bus every morning and then pick him up every afternoon."[66]

Despite these duties, Mrs. Kim also worked as a volunteer. She taught dressmaking at the local YWCA and she organized a group of Korean women to make clothes for poor women's babies. She also volunteered at the local public library. She explained, "Every Wednesday afternoon, about fifteen of us visit [the library] to read books to the children who have to pass their time in the library after school hours because their mothers are working. Some of the children want us to read English books, and others want Korean books. We read whatever they want. The children like us."[67]

Kim also studied English in adult education classes and made friends with a Thai student who told her about classes offered through city college. Mrs. Kim declared, "I never knew that an old lady like me could go to college. . . . I am happy with my life in America. I feel that I have been blessed."[68]

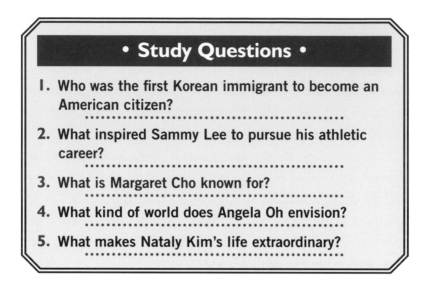

• Study Questions •

1. Who was the first Korean immigrant to become an American citizen?

2. What inspired Sammy Lee to pursue his athletic career?

3. What is Margaret Cho known for?

4. What kind of world does Angela Oh envision?

5. What makes Nataly Kim's life extraordinary?

10

Conclusion

In a fairly short period of time, Korean immigrants have made their mark on American society. This narrative spans the entire twentieth century and involves the histories of both Korea and the United States. It is a remarkable journey—one that includes some of the darkest chapters of American history.

In many ways, the Korean immigrant experience is the typical American story—immigrants from another land who sacrifice to make a better life for their families and who believe in the promise and opportunity that America offers. It is different, however, in that, despite the common immigrant struggle of settling into a new country, the majority of European immigrants did not face the kinds of racial discrimination that Asian immigrants did in the nineteenth and twentieth centuries.

This is especially true for the first wave of Korean immigrants who, in spite of racial discrimination, legal exclusion,

Although Korean Americans have established themselves in the United States, their bond to their homeland remains strong. Pictured here is a group of Korean-American children waving the flags of both the United States and South Korea during a 2003 rally in Los Angeles against the development of nuclear weapons in North Korea.

and limited opportunities, built thriving communities in Hawaii and on the mainland, which would ultimately become the foundation for post-1965 immigration. In a world that was hostile to Asians, these early Korean immigrants were true pioneers. They were the first Korean immigrants to attend college, establish businesses, and so on. At the same time, as they established their lives in America, they could not forget Korea. The political activities of Korean immigrants through the Korean independence movement demonstrates how immigrants can be American and still maintain ties to their homeland.

When we consider Korean immigration, the experiences of Korean adoptees reveal a "hidden history," but they also show

how the experiences of war and the historic ties between the United States and Korea shape migration in unexpected ways. At the same time, the experiences of Korean adoptees also suggest the ways in which American identities are formed and transformed.

Post-1965 Korean immigration has transformed both the United States and Canada in significant ways. Korean immigrants have come to dominate specific industries, such as nail salons, green grocers, liquor stores, convenience stores, and wig shops. Korean immigrants have also built thriving Koreatowns that provide a whole range of services for Korean immigrants.

At the same time, events such as the 1992 Los Angeles riots make it clear that immigrant communities cannot isolate themselves from American society. Korean immigrants have learned, perhaps painfully, that participating in the American political process and building alliances with other racial groups is essential for the well-being of Korean communities in the United States. This is a useful lesson for all Americans, especially as America becomes increasingly multiracial.

Korean immigration is an American immigrant story. It is a story of struggle and sacrifice. It is a story of success and achievement. Finally, it is an unfinished story to which new chapters will be added with continuing Korean immigration and the emergence of new generations of Korean Americans.

Chronology

1882 Chinese Exclusion Act, banning Chinese laborers from entering the United States, is passed by Congress; United States officially establishes diplomatic relations with Korea when the two nations sign the Treaty of Peace, Amity, Commerce and Navigation.

1890 Philip Jaisohn becomes the first Korean to obtain U.S. citizenship.

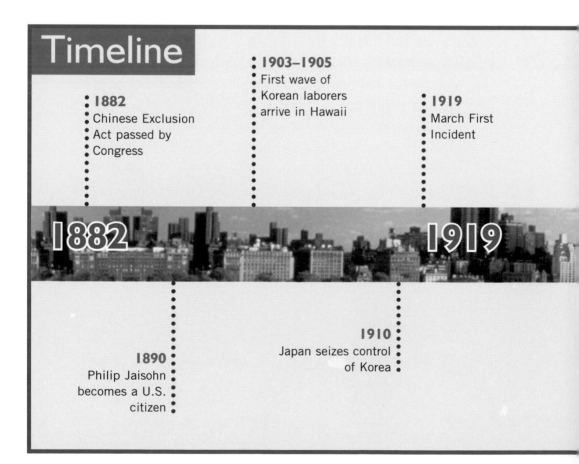

Timeline

1882
Chinese Exclusion Act passed by Congress

1903–1905
First wave of Korean laborers arrive in Hawaii

1919
March First Incident

1882   1919

1890
Philip Jaisohn becomes a U.S. citizen

1910
Japan seizes control of Korea

1903–1905 First wave of Korean laborers (approximately 7,000) immigrate to Hawaii.

1904 The First Korean immigrant church is established in Hawaii.

1907 Gentlemen's Agreement is signed between Japan and the United States, which halts the immigration of Japanese laborers; this affects Koreans because after Japanese colonization of Korea in 1910, they are considered Japanese nationals.

1910 Japan colonizes Korea.

1910–1924 Korean "picture brides" continue to enter the United States.

1919 March First Incident, the peaceful, mass demonstration by Koreans against Japanese colonial rule, occurs.

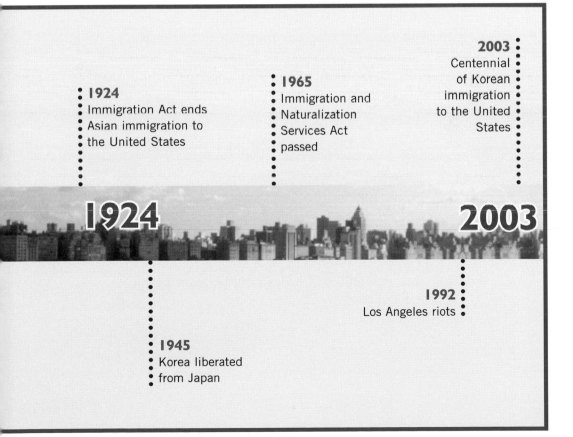

1924
Immigration Act ends Asian immigration to the United States

1965
Immigration and Naturalization Services Act passed

2003
Centennial of Korean immigration to the United States

1924   2003

1992
Los Angeles riots

1945
Korea liberated from Japan

1924	Immigration Act effectively ends Asian immigration to the United States by closing off the loophole for "picture brides."
1940	Korean-American population reaches 8,568.
1941	Internment of Japanese Americans; Koreans, despite their status as Japanese nationals, are exempt.
1945	World War II ends with the defeat of Japan; Korea is liberated.
1948	Korea is divided into North and South Korea at the 38th Parallel; Sammy Lee becomes the first Asian American to win an Olympic gold medal for the United States when he brings home the first of two gold medals in Olympic 10-meter platform diving.
1950–1953	Korean War occurs, with the Soviet Union and the United States participating.
1950s	Korean adoptions begin in the United States.
1965	Immigration and Naturalization Services Act relaunches mass Korean immigration.
1992	Los Angeles riots take place from April 29 to May 4; Jay Kim becomes the first Korean American elected to Congress when he wins the 41st District seat in California.
1994	Margaret Cho wins the American Comedy Award for Best Female Comedian.
1997	Kim Jong-il becomes leader of North Korea; Angela Oh appointed to President Clinton's Initiative on Race.
2003	The centennial of Korean immigration to the United States.

Notes

Chapter 1

1. Mary Paik Lee, *Quiet Odyssey: A Pioneer Korean Woman in America* (Seattle, Wash.: University of Washington Press, 1990), 12.

2. Henry George, "The Chinese in California," *New York Tribune*, May 1, 1869. Reprinted in Lon Kurashige and Alice Yang Murray, eds., *Major Problems in Asian American History* (New York: Houghton Mifflin, 2003), 99.

3. *Proceedings of the Asiatic Exclusion League, 1907–1913.* Reprinted in Lon Kurashige and Alice Yang Murray, eds., *Major Problems in Asian American History* (New York: Houghton Mifflin, 2003), 113.

Chapter 2

4. Bruce Cummings, *Korea's Place in the Sun: A Modern History* (New York: W.W. Norton, 1997), 55.

5. Louise Yim, *My Forty Year Fight for Korea* (New York: A.A. Wyn, 1959), 81.

6. Quoted in Takaki, *Strangers From a Different Shore*, 54–55.

7. "North Koreans Forced to Eat Grass," BBC News, June 20, 2002. Available online at *http://news.bbc.co.uk/1/hi/world/asia-pacific/2055658.stm.*

8. Doug Struck, "Opening a Window on North Korea's Horrors," *Washington Post,* October 3, 2003. Available online at *http://www.washingtonpost.com/ac2/wp-dyn/A41966-2003Oct3?language=printer.*

9. "In Pictures: Korean Family Reunions," BBC World News, April 29, 2002. Available online at *http://news.bbc.co.uk/2/hi/asia-pacific/1957844.stm.*

Chapter 3

10. Alice Chai, "A Picture Bride from Korea: The Life History of a Korean American Woman in Hawai'i," *Bridge* (Winter 1978): 37. Quoted in Ronald Takaki, *Strangers From a Different Shore: A History of Asian Americans* (Boston: Little, Brown, 1990), 56.

11. Ibid., 54.

12. Ibid., 55.

13. Sucheng Chan, introduction to Mary Paik Lee, *Quiet Odyssey: A Pioneer Korean Woman in America* (Seattle, Wash.: University of Washington Press, 1990), xlviii.

Chapter 4

14. Sonia Shinn Sunoo, *Korea Kaleidoscope: Early Korean Pioneers in the USA, Oral Histories, vol. 1*. Sierra Mission Area, United Presbyterian Church, 1982, 3.

15. Easurk Emsen Charr, *The Golden Mountain: The Autobiography of a Korean Immigrant, 1895–1960* (Urbana, Ill.: University of Illinois Press, 1996), 139–140.

16. Ibid., 140.

17. Quoted in Takaki, *Strangers From a Different Shore*, 290.

18. Soo-young Chin, *Doing What Had to Be Done: The Life Narrative of Dora Yum Kim* (Philadelphia, Pa.: Temple University Press, 1999), 51.

19. Ibid., 44.

20. Ibid., 52–53.

21. Peter Hyun, *In the New World: The Making of a Korean American* (Honolulu, Hawaii: University of Hawaii Press, 1991), 189–190.

22. Ibid., 56.

23. Ibid., 55.

Chapter 5

24. Eun-Young Kim, "Career Choice Among Second-generation Korean Americans: Reflections of a Cultural Model of Success," *Anthropology and Education Quarterly* 24, no. 3 (1993): 229.

25. Min-Jung Kwak, "Work in Family Business and Gender Relations: A Case Study of Recent Korean Immigrant Women." University of British Columbia, unpublished paper, 2002, 3.

26. Ibid., 4.

27. Ibid., 14.

28. Ibid., 21.

29. Ibid., 21.

30. Ibid. 18.

Chapter 6

31. Elaine Kim and Eui-young Kim, *East to America: Korean American Life Stories* (New York: New Press, 1996), 307.

32. Ibid., 310.

33. Ibid., 312.

34. "A Reunion Revisited," *Adoption Today*. Available online at *http://www.adopting.org/AdoptionToday/ReunionRevisited.html*.

35. Mirim Kim, "Seoul Searching: A Korean-American Adoptee Visits Her Former Homeland," Adopted Korean Connection.com. Available online at *http://www.akconnection.com/stories/mirim.asp?cat=4*.

36. Soo-ji Min, "Home Away From Seoul: An Examination of Korean Adoption," *Asian Week* (August 13, 2003): 16.

Chapter 7

37. Kim and Kim, *East to America*, 39.

38. Ibid.

39. Ella Stewart, "Communication Between African Americans and Korean Americans: Before and After the Los Angeles

Riots," in E. Chang and R. Leong, eds., *Los Angeles— Struggles Toward Multiethnic Community* (Seattle, Wash.: University of Washington Press, 1994), 40.

40. Anna Deavere Smith, *Twilight Los Angeles 1992* (New York: Anchor Books, 1994), 245.

41. Kim and Kim, *East to America*, 248.

42. Ibid., 349.

Chapter 8

43. Kim and Kim, *East to America*, 182–183.

44. Ibid., 210.

45. Ibid., 84.

46. Ibid., 210.

47. Ibid., 84–85.

48. JeeYeun Lee, "A Preliminary Needs Assessment of 1.5 and Second Generation Korean Americans in the Chicago Area," Korean American Community Services Report (June 2003), 15.

49. Ibid., 10.

50. Ibid., 13.

51. Sandhya Somashekhar, "Abuse in the Land of Promise," *Washington Post* (October 6, 2005).

52. Ibid.

53. Ibid.

54. Kim and Kim, *East to America*, 144.

55. Ibid., 344.

56. Ibid., 333.

Chapter 9

57. Chin, *Doing What Had to Be Done*, 3.

58. Ibid., 98.

59. Ibid., 131–132.

60. Erika Cheng, "Dr. Sammy Lee: The Elder Statesman of Olympic Diving," The Asians in America Project. Available online at *http://www.asiansi namerica.org/museum/1204_ museum.html*.

61. Ibid.

62. Margaret Cho, "General Bio," November 11, 2005. Available online at *http://margaretcho. net/biography/general.htm*.

63. Ibid.

64. "What Happened to the National Race Dialogue?: An Interview with Angela Oh," *Colorlines* 2, no. 2 (Summer 1999): 24.

65. Ibid.

66. Kim and Kim, *East to America*, 272.

67. Ibid.

68. Ibid., 273.

Glossary

affirmative action   Dating to the 1960s, an effort was made by the U.S. government to address inequalities resulting from discrimination in employment and higher education. Korean immigrants, like other Asian immigrants, women, and other racial minorities benefit tremendously in the 1970s and 1980s.

Chinese Exclusion Act (1882)   Signed into law in 1882, this act forbade Chinese laborers from entering the United States and was passed in response to massive anti-Chinese sentiment on the West Coast that perceived Chinese as economic competitors. It was the first time in U.S. history that a group was excluded purely by racial or ethnic category. The act was not repealed until 1943, when China became a U.S. wartime ally.

Communism   A form of political and social organization that calls for common ownership, generally by the government, of property and the means of production and equitable distribution of goods among all citizens to achieve an equitable and just society.

Confucianism   A belief system that provides a clear guide for all relationships: between rulers and subjects, husbands and wives, parents and children, and elders and youth. It places an emphasis on proper and harmonious social relationships in all aspects of life, including government, the legal system, the family, and society. Until the nineteenth century, Confucianism allowed Korea to maintain a stable sociopolitical system on the North Asian peninsula, as well as, in general, peaceful relations with her more powerful neighbors.

Democratic Peoples Republic of Korea   Present-day North Korea.

Gentlemen's Agreement (1907)   An accord between the United States and Japan, whereby Japan stopped issuing passports to laborers. It was the result of anti-Japanese sentiment on the West Coast that perceived Japanese immigrants to be an economic threat. Unlike the 1882 Chinese

Exclusion Act, which singled out the Chinese by name, the United States could not treat Japan in the same way, given Japan's status as a world power. It ultimately included Korean immigrants after the colonization of Korea by Japan in 1910.

Immigration Act of 1924   This Congressional act established a quota system for immigration; allowed for 2 percent of population from a specific country already present according to the 1890 U.S. census. It was designed to limit eastern and southern European immigration, which only began in significant numbers after 1890, and to encourage immigration from western Europe. Also closed off any remaining loopholes (for example, picture brides) that allowed for Asian immigration.

Immigration and Naturalization Services Act of 1965
Abolished national quota system established by Immigration Act of 1924 and instead established a number of visas for those living in the Western and Eastern Hemisphere. It also gave preference to family reunification, which allowed individuals already in the United States to invite immediate family members to join them. Also provided for entry of professionals whose services were needed in the United States, especially in the fields of nursing and technology. It also relaunched mass Asian immigration.

Korean War   Civil war (1950–1953) between Communist North and pro-democracy South Korea. After division of Korea into North and South Korea, at the 38th parallel, following World War II, tensions escalated on the Korean Peninsula. On June 25, 1950, North Korea invaded South Korea. To help stem the tide of Communism in Asia as China joined the North Korean war effort, the United States entered the war in support of South Korea. A cease-fire was declared in 1953, but to date, no peace treaty has been signed.

kyes   Rotating credit associations used by Koreans and other immigrants to provide access to money to start businesses and purchase property. Kyes have been critical to Korean immigrant entrepreneurship. Many recent immigrants face difficulties in borrowing money from a bank, because they lack credit histories and they have lived in the United States only a short time.

Los Angeles riots (1992)   In April 1992, after four white Los Angeles police officers were declared innocent for the violent beating of Rodney King, a black man, people took to the streets and three days of civil unrest began. Hostilities between blacks and whites in Los Angeles had occurred for a long time, but in 1992, Koreans became caught in the crossfire as many of their stores were looted and burned. Korean businesses suffered more than $4 million in damages.

March First Incident   Peaceful mass demonstration held in Korea March 1, 1919, during the colonial period. It began a significant period of overseas Korean independence activity.

model minority   First surfaced in the media in the 1960s to refer to the successes of Asian immigrant communities, in contrast to other minority groups, including Latinos and African Americans. Low levels of crime, high numbers of college graduates, and higher incomes are used to define the group.

picture brides   Established in the early part of the twentieth century to allow single Korean and Japanese men to marry, at a time when Japanese and Korean laborers were prohibited from entering the United States due to the 1907 Gentlemen's Agreement. The law left a loophole open for wives and families of Japanese and Korean immigrant men already in America to enter the United States. Thus, potential brides exchanged photos with their prospective husbands, and the couple was "married" in Korea or Japan by having the bride's name entered in the husband's family register. Once married, these picture brides could apply for passports to join their husbands in America. The picture bride system allowed for the emigration of more than 20,000 Japanese and 1,200 Korean women in the first two decades of the twentieth century. The loophole was eliminated by the Immigration Act of 1924.

Republic of Korea   Present-day South Korea.

Tangun   Founder of Korea in 2333 B.C.

Bibliography

Cha, Kyung-Cha. *Pumpkin Flower and Patriotism.* Los Angeles: Korean American Research Center, 1991.

Charr, Easurk Emsen. *The Golden Mountain: The Autobiography of a Korean Immigrant, 1895–1960.* Urbana, Ill.: University of Illinois Press, 1996.

Cheng, Erika. "Dr. Sammy Lee: The Elder Statesman of Olympic Diving," The Asians in America Project. Available online at *http://www.asiansinamerica.org/museum/1204_museum.html.*

Chin, Soo-young. *Doing What Had to Be Done: The Life Narrative of Dora Yum Kim.* Philadelphia, Pa.: Temple University Press, 1999.

Cho, Margaret. "General Bio." Available online at *http://margaretcho. net/biography/general.htm.*

Cummings, Bruce. *Korea's Place in the Sun: A Modern History.* New York: W.W. Norton, 1997.

Daniels, Cora. "Ji Baek Rescue Salons," CNN Money.com. Available online at *http://money.cnn.com/magazines/fsb/fsb_archive/2003/1 2/01/359902/index.htm.* Updated on December 1, 2003.

George, Henry. "The Chinese in California." *New York Tribune,* May 1, 1869. Reprinted in Lon Kurashige and Alice Yang Murray, eds. *Major Problems in Asian American History.* New York: Houghton Mifflin, 2003.

Hyun, Peter. *In the New World: The Making of a Korean American.* Honolulu, Hawaii: University of Hawaii Press, 1991.

"In Pictures: Korean Family Reunions," BBC World News. Available online at *http://news.bbc.co.uk/2/hi/asia-pacific/1957844.stm.* Updated April 29, 2002.

Kang, Miliann. "The Managed Hand: The Commercialization of Bodies and Emotions in Korean Immigrant-owned Nail Salons." *Gender and Society* 17: p. 6.

Kim, Elaine, and Eui-young Kim. *East to America: Korean American Life Stories.* New York: New Press, 1996.

Kim, Eun-Young. "Career Choice Among Second-generation Korean Americans: Reflections of a Cultural Model of Success." *Anthropology and Education Quarterly* 24 (1993): p. 3.

Kim, Mirim, "Seoul Searching: A Korean-American Adoptee Visits Her Former Homeland," Adopted Korean Connection.com. Available online at *http://www.akconnection.com/stories/mirim. asp?cat=4.*

Kwak, Min-Jung. "Work in Family Business and Gender Relations: A Case Study of Recent Korean Immigrant Women." University of British Columbia, unpublished paper, 2002. Available online at *www.uoguelph.ca/cfww/resources/ attachments/Min-Jung%20Kwak.pdf.*

Lee, Jee Yeun. "A Preliminary Needs Assessment of 1.5 and Second Generation Korean Americans in the Chicago Area," Korean American Community Services. Available online at *www.kacschgo. org/files/report.pdf.* June 2003.

Lee, Mary Paik. *Quiet Odyssey: A Pioneer Korean Woman in America.* Seattle, Wash.: University of Washington Press, 1990.

Min, Soo-ji. "Home Away From Seoul: An Examination of Korean Adoption." *Asian Week.* (August 13, 2003): p. 16.

"North Koreans Forced to Eat Grass," BBC News. Available online at *http://news.bbc.co.uk/1/hi/world/asia-pacific/2055658.stm.* June 20, 2002.

Proceedings of the Asiatic Exclusion League, 1907–1913. Reprinted in Lon Kurashige and Alice Yang Murray, ed. *Major Problems in Asian American History.* New York: Houghton Mifflin, 2003, p. 113.

"A Reunion Revisited," Adoption Today. Available online at *http:// www.adopting.org/AdoptionToday/ReunionRevisited.html.*

Smith, Anna Deavere. *Twilight Los Angeles 1992.* New York: Anchor Books, 1994.

Somashekhar, Sandhya. "Abuse in the Land of Promise." *Washington Post,* October 6, 2005.

Stewart, Ella. "Communication Between African Americans and Korean Americans: Before and After the Los Angeles Riots."

In E. Chang and R. Leong, eds. *Los Angeles—Struggles Toward Multiethnic Community.* Seattle, Wash.: University of Washington Press, 1994.

Struck, Doug. "Opening a Window on North Korea's Horrors." *Washington Post.* Available online at *http://www.washingtonpost.com/ac2/wp-dyn/A41966-2003Oct3?language=printer.* October 3, 2003.

Sunoo, Sonia Shinn. *Korea Kaleidoscope: Early Korean Pioneers in the USA, Oral Histories, vol. 1.* Sierra Mission Area, United Presbyterian Church, 1982.

Takaki, Ronald. *Strangers From a Different Shore: A History of Asian Americans.* Boston: Little, Brown, 1989.

Terry, Don. "Decades of Rage Created Crucible of Violence." *New York Times,* May 3, 1992.

The Wanderer: The Story of Reverend Sang-chul Lee. A Scattering of Seeds: the Creation of Canada. Available online at *http://www.whitepinepictures.com/seeds/ii/24/index.html.*

"What Happened to the National Race Dialogue?: An Interview With Angela Oh." *Colorlines* 2, no. 2 (Summer 1999): p. 24.

Yim, Louise. *My Forty Year Fight for Korea.* New York: A.A. Wyn, 1959.

Further Reading

Chin, Soo-Young. *Doing What Had to Be Done: The Life Narrative of Dora Yum Kim.* Philadelphia, Pa.: Temple University Press, 1999.

Kang, K. Connie. *Home Was the Land of the Morning Calm: A Saga of a Korean–American Family.* Cambridge, Mass.: Da Capo Press, 2003.

Kang, Younghill. *East Goes West.* New York: Scribner and Sons, 1937.

Kim, Elaine, and Eui-young Yu. *East to American: Korean American Life Stories.* New York: New Press, 1997.

Kim, Richard E. *Lost Names: Scenes From a Korean Boyhood.* Berkeley and Los Angeles: University of California Press, 1998.

Kim, Ronyoung. *Clay Walls.* Sag Harbor, N.Y.: Permanent Press, 1996.

Lee, Maria. *Necessary Roughness.* New York: Harper Collins, 1996.

Lee, Mary Paik. *Quiet Odyssey: A Pioneer Korean Woman in America.* Seattle, Wash.: University of Washington Press, 1990.

Na, An. *A Step From Heaven.* Asheville, N.C.: Front Street, 2001.

——. *Wait for Me.* New York: Putnam, 2006.

Takaki, Ronald. *Strangers From a Different Shore.* Boston: Little, Brown, 1989.

Trenka, Jane Jeong. *The Language of Blood: A Memoir.* St. Paul, Minn.: Borealis Books, 2003.

WEB SITES

Philip Jaisohn Memorial Foundation
http://www.jaisohn.org

Korean American Historical Society
www.kahs.org

The Los Angeles Korean Community
http://www.msmc.la.edu/ccf/LAC.Korean.html

National Association of Korean Americans
http://www.naka.org/

Picture Credits

Index

A

adoption. *See* Korean adoptees
affirmative action, 96–97
African Americans
    aftermath of Los Angeles riots
      and, 58–59, 72, 73, 77–80,
      105–107
    background of Los Angeles
      riots and, 57–58, 73, 74–76
    business loans to, 76
    unemployment of, 75
agriculture
    in California, 45–46
    success in, 46
    sugarcane industry, 12, 13,
      35–36, 38–39, 41
Ahn Chang-ho, 50
Ahn Cuddy, Susan, 50–51
All-American Girl, 103
American Civil Liberties Union
    award, 105
American Comedy Award for Best
    Female Comedian, 103
Asian Americans, discrimination
    against, 15, 16
Asian immigrants
    discrimination against, 36,
      42
    distinguishing among, 14
    limiting entry, 16–19
    as model minority, 92, 93
Asiatic Exclusion League, 18
Assassin, 105
assimilation, 66, 67, 70
    See also culture
athletes, 102–103
awards, 61, 103, 105

B

Baek, Ji, 86–87
belief systems, 22, 23
"big brother-little brother"
    relationship, 22
Bishop, Janice, 66–67, 69
Bourke, Gerald, 29
boycotts, 75
Buddhism, 22, 23
Bush, George W., 31

C

California
    agricultural industry in, 45–46
    awards, 50
    Korean population in 1940, 15
    political involvement in, 79
    racial discrimination before
      1965 in, 44–45, 46–47,
      102–103
    self-employment in, 55
Canada, 59–62
Cha, Kyung-Soo, 15
Charr, Easurk Emsen, 45
Children Placement Services, 64
China
    defeated by Japan, 23
    exiled Korean government in,
      26
    influence on Korea of, 22, 23
    North Korea and, 26, 28
Chinese Exclusion Act (1882),
    17–18
Chinese immigrants
    as contract laborers, 38
    exclusion of, 16–18
Cho, Margaret, 103, 105

Christianity
    churches, 40–41, 85
    missionaries, 38–39, 59
    in South Korea, 30
citizenship
    denial of, 14
    first Korean obtained, 99
civil rights movement, 57
Clinton, Bill, 79, 106
cold war, 26
comedians, 103, 105
Communism, 26, 28
Confucianism, 22, 23
contract laborers, 38
credit associations, 88
criminal activity, 94
culture
    Confucianism and, 23
    export of Korean, 31
    under Japanese rule, 24
    Koreatowns and, 82–83
    maintaining, 42, 47–49
    maintaining among adoptees,
        67, 68, 71
    maintaining through churches,
        85
    sports, 30–31

D

defectors, 29
demilitarized zone (DMZ), 28
Democratic Republic of Korea. *See*
    North Korea
discrimination. *See* racial
    discrimination
diving, 102, 103
domestic violence, 92–94
downward mobility, 90
Du, Soon Ja, 75

E

education
    in Canada, 59
    level of immigrants, 84, 87
    of second-generation Koreans,
        42, 85–86

enemy alien classification, 14
entrepreneurship
    in Canada, 59, 60–62
    family life and, 90–91
    funding businesses, 88
    in Los Angeles, 73–74, 76–77
    of post-1965 immigrants, 55
    racial discrimination and, 46
    success in, 83–86
    women, 86–87
ethnic identity. *See* culture

F

family businesses. *See* self-
    employment
family life
    reunification in United States,
        55
    reunions of North and South
        Koreans, 31
    self-employment and, 90–91
    violence in, 92–94
famine
    in colonial Korea, 37
    in North Korea, 28–29
First Amendment Award, 105
food, 47

G

gangs, 94
Gentlemen's Agreement (1907), 18,
    33, 36
George, Henry, 16–17
Gojong (king of Korea), 25
Gojoseon, 21–22
"Grandma Holt," 64

H

Harlins, Latasha, 75–76
Hawaii
    early immigration to, 12, 13
    isolation of Korean immigrants
        in, 40–41
    Korean population in 1940,
        14–15

laborers in sugar plantations,
35–36, 38–39
maintaining culture in, 42
picture brides in, 34–35
racial discrimination in,
41–42
Hawaiian Sugar Planters'
Association (HSPA), 38, 40
Hee, Park Chung, 30
Hermit Kingdom, 22
Holt, Bertha, 64
Holt, Henry, 64
Holt International, 64
"homecoming visits," 68–70
Hwanung (son of heaven), 21

I

identity
of Korean adoptees, 70, 110–
111
of second-generation Koreans,
48–49
See also culture
I'm the One That I Want, 105
immigration
after 1965, 19, 54, 55
to Canada, 59–62
challenges to success of, 89–90
during 1950s, 55
number of Koreans from 1952–
2004, 12
number of Koreans from 1998–
2004, 56
picture bride system and,
33–35
quotas, 18–19
reasons for, 12, 35, 36–39
status of Korean immigrants,
14, 18
working class, 87–88, 96–97
See also Korean adoptees
Immigration Act (1924), 18–19
Immigration and Naturalization
Services Act (1965), 19, 54,
55
Independence Club, 99

Initiative on Race, 79, 106
international adoption, 63–65

J

Jaisohn, Philip, 98–101
Japan
Korea as colony of, 13, 14–15,
23–25, 36–37
as world power, 18, 23
Japanese Americans, 50
Japanese immigrants
as contract laborers, 38
exclusion of, 18
marriage of, 33–34
Jones, George Heber, 40
Joseon Dynasty, 22, 23

K

Kim, Debby, 101
Kim, Dora Yum, 101–102
Kim, Jay, 79
Kim, Mirim, 70
Kim, Nataly, 107–108
Kim, Tom, 101
Kim Chong-nim, 46
Kim Il Sung, 28
Kim Jong-il, 28
King, Rodney, 58, 73
Koguryo, 22
Korea
as colony of Japan, 13, 14–15,
23–25, 36–37
"homecoming visits" for
adoptees, 68–70
independence movement,
25–26
independence movement in
United States, 15, 41, 47–48,
99–100
independence of, 19
influence of China on, 22,
23
legendary founding of, 21
liberation of, 26, 49
modernization of, 99
returning to, 47, 99

See also North Korea; South
    Korea
Korean adoptees
    annual number of, 64
    assimilation of, 66, 67
    demand for, 64–66
    "homecoming visits," 68–70
    identity of, 70, 110–111
    racial discrimination and,
        66–67
Korean Overseas Compatriots Prize,
    61
Korean Review (magazine), 99
Korean War
    aftermath of, 28
    children of American soldiers,
        64–65
    cold war and, 26
    orphans, 64
Koreatowns, 73, 82–83
kyes, 88

L

La Choy Food Products, 47
laborers
    contract, 38
    in sugar plantations, 35–36,
        38–39
language schools, 47, 48
Latinos
    Korean businesses and, 73
    Los Angeles riots and, 72, 76
    unemployment of, 75
Lee, Mary Paik, 11–12
Lee, Sammy, 102–103
Lee, Sang-Chul, 61
legends, 21
Los Angeles, 1992 riots
    aftermath of, 58–59, 72, 73,
        77–80, 105–107
    background of, 57–58, 73,
        74–76

M

March First Movement (1919),
    25–26

marriage
    picture bride system, 33–35
    of second-generation Koreans,
        48–49
    war brides, 55
media, 74
Methodist missionaries, 40
Min-ja Sur, 25
missionaries
    immigration to Canada and, 59
    immigration to U.S. and,
        38–39, 40
model minority thesis, 92, 93
multiculturalism, 66, 71, 78, 79–80,
    95–96
multiracial riots. *See* Los Angeles,
    1992 riots
myths, 21

N

nail salons, 86–87
New, Ilhan, 47
New York City, 55
North Korea, 26, 28–30, 31
Notorious C.H.O., 105
nursing, 55, 101

O

occupations
    in agriculture, 35–36, 38–39,
        45–46
    Asians as source of cheap labor,
        16, 18
    professional, 42, 55, 57, 105–
        107
    See also self-employment
Oh, Angela, 79, 105–107

P

Paekche, 22
peaches, fuzzless, 46
picture bride system, 33–35
platform diving, 102, 103
political involvement, 59, 79–80,
    105–107
Presbyterian missionaries, 40

Q
quota system, 18–19

R
racial discrimination
    affirmative action and, 96–97
    against Asian Americans, 15, 16
    against Asian immigrants, 36,
        42
    in California, 44–45, 46–47,
        102–103
    in Hawaii, 41–42
    Korean adoptees and, 66–67
    maintaining cultural identity
        and, 48
    by minorities, 76–77, 95–96
    model minority thesis and,
        92, 93
    second-generation Koreans
        and, 94–95
    self-employment and, 46
    World War II and, 51
religion
    importance of churches, 40–41
    missionaries, 38–39, 40, 59
    in South Korea, 30
    See also Confucianism
Republic of Korea. See South Korea
Rescue Beauty saloons, 86–87
Revolution, 105
Rhee, Syngman, 30, 41
riots. See Los Angeles, 1992 riots
rotating credit associations, 88
Russia, 23
Russo-Japanese War (1905), 23

S
sa-i-gu, 72
    See also Los Angeles, 1992 riots
second-generation Koreans
    civil rights movement and, 57
    educational achievements of,
        42, 85–86
    in Hawaii, 41–42
    identity of, 48–49
    maintenance of culture and, 42

    political activism of, 79–80,
        105–107
    as professionals, 42
    racial discrimination and, 48,
        94–95
    stresses on, 90–92
self-employment
    in Canada, 59, 60–62
    funding businesses, 88
    in Los Angeles, 73–74, 76–77
    of post-1965 immigrants, 55
    racial discrimination and, 46
    sacrifices and, 90–91
    success in, 83–86
    women entrepreneurs, 86–87
Seoul, Korea, 25
Silla, 22
Sino-Japanese War (1895), 23
Smith, Wallace, 47
social mobility
    downward, 90
    of second-generation Koreans,
        85–86
    of working-class immigrants,
        87–88, 96–97
Soh Chae Pil, 98–101
South Central Los Angeles. See Los
    Angeles, 1992 riots
South Korea
    cultural exports of, 30–31
    established, 26
    first president, 41
    Korean War and, 28
    North Korean defectors to, 29
Soviet Union, 26, 28
sports, 30–31, 102–103
S.S. Gaelic, 35
sugar plantations, 12, 13, 35–36,
    38–39, 41
swimming, 102
Switzer, Suzanne, 69–70

T
Tangun (Korean leader), 21
38th parallel, 26
Thompson, Walter, 75

Three Kingdoms, 22, 23
Toronto, Canada, 59, 62

U

United Nations, 26, 29
United States
    children of soldiers and Korean
        women, 64–65
    Korea independence movement
        in, 15, 41, 47–48, 99–100
    Korean immigrants admitted
        1952–2004, 12
    Korean population before
        1965, 44
    Korean population by state, 83
    Korean population currently,
        54
    Korean War and, 26, 28
    limiting entry of Asian
        immigrants, 16–19
    Navy, 50–51
    occupation of South Korea
        by, 30
    reasons for success in, 83–86

V

Vancouver, Canada, 59, 62

violence, 45
    See also Los Angeles, 1992 riots

W

war brides, 55
women
    children of American soldiers
        and Korean, 64–65
    comedians, 103, 105
    community leaders, 101–102
    employment in family
        businesses, 60–62
    entrepreneurs, 86–87
    political activists, 79, 105–107
    in U.S. Navy, 50–51
World War II
    liberation of Korea, 26
    opportunities during, 51–52
    patriotism during, 49–50
    status of Korean immigrants
        and, 14
    women in U.S. Navy, 50–51

Y

Youngman, Park, 41
youth gangs, 94
Yuhan Corporation, 47

About the Contributors

Series Editor **Robert D. Johnston** is associate professor and director of the Teaching of History Program in the Department of History at the University of Illinois at Chicago. He is the author of *The Making of America: The History of the United States from 1492 to the Present*, a middle-school textbook that received a *School Library Journal* Best Book of the Year award. He is currently working on a history of vaccine controversies in American history, to be published by Oxford University Press.

Anne Soon Choi is assistant professor of American Studies at the University of Kansas. Her research interests include explorations of American empire, U.S. Immigration, and the global circulation of political ideology.